SpringerBriefs in Electrical and Computer Engineering

For further volumes:
http://www.springer.com/series/10059

Peter J. Morales · Dennis Anderson

Process Simulation and Parametric Modeling for Strategic Project Management

Foreword by Beth Ouellette

 Springer

Peter J. Morales
School of Law
New York University
New York, NY
USA

Dennis Anderson
St. Francis College
Brooklyn, NY
USA

ISSN 2191-8112   ISSN 2191-8120   (electronic)
ISBN 978-1-4614-6988-9   ISBN 978-1-4614-6989-6   (eBook)
DOI 10.1007/978-1-4614-6989-6
Springer New York Heidelberg Dordrecht London

Library of Congress Control Number: 2013936971

Printed on acid-free paper

Springer is part of Springer Science+Business Media (www.springer.com)

Foreword

Value Framework is an important, significant underlying set of ideas, principles, agreements or rules, which provide a basis for an outline which is intended to be more fully developed at a later stage, providing usefulness to the organization.

B. Ouellette

What if you could predict the ultimate successful outcome of your organization's strategic intention? Wouldn't your value to the organization instantly become exponentially greater? Of course it would; therefore, you need to implement the Value Framework as authors outline in *Process Simulation and Parametric Modeling for Strategic Project Management*.

We have seen projects and project management improving through the years, yet the constant challenge we face is ensuring that they are still valid and will still add value upon their completion. Two key components of this are (1) alignment with objectives and (2) continuous engagement of stakeholders.

Throughout *Process Simulation and Parametric Modeling for Strategic Project Management* a "Value Framework" is introduced as a way to compare potential project choices. Thus, a leap of faith is taken to move away from the more traditional ROI-based analysis for project justification, posing that a traditional ROI system can become an artificial construct where the future project benefits are converted into dollar value based on revenue generated or costs avoided. The authors agree that while this does have merit, there are potentially equally important measures of strategic value which are hard, if not impossible, to quantify as revenue. However, revenue can be one of the elements in a Value Framework.

We often have stakeholder engagement on the front end of a project, or perhaps on the back end—just in time to take credit for the success. But lacking is active stakeholder participation throughout the project. Similarly, we see that there is often much work done on the front end of a project to document its alignment with one or more strategic objectives. After all, part of the business case requires us to check the box that says "Project A is aligned with Strategy Q." So the box is checked, and we are off and running to manage the project. Yet when the project completes, it may, or may not actually support the current strategic objectives. As you are walked through several examples of a process for defining a Value

Framework common to the stakeholders, you will be shown how developing this framework at the beginning of the discussion process will actually bond stakeholders together in ways that would not normally happen. Working with the stakeholders of a project from this starting point is a critical step to build a strong foundation for stakeholder engagement and maintain it throughout the project.

Strategic Project Management requires continuous and complete alignment with strategic objectives throughout the life of the project and active, continuous, visible stakeholder engagement throughout the life of the project. These are the secret ingredients toward success. Sounds simple right? So why isn't everyone doing it? It is not being done, largely because they do not know how to do it. You are given a recipe for success as you move from chapter to chapter. The authors give you the process and tools to do this in a hands-on, concrete way. The first step of this is to use the Value Framework for alignment. The second step is to clarify options and prioritize, and the third step is to implement. To increase the probability of success long-term, there must be continued alignment of projects and programs with the strategy and supporting objectives alongside of continued stakeholder engagement.

Throughout the book, there is clear emphasis on the core tentacles of this book: quantify a strategic alignment between projects and organization direction, optimize the selection of the project portfolio—while considering both risk and strategic value, and perform agile project estimation based on a discrete event simulation.

Chapters at a Glance:

Chapter 1 sets the foundation and clarifies that projects are investments and they must be aligned with the strategic intention of the organization.

Chapter 2 steps you through precisely "how" to optimize the project investment portfolio through strategic alignment. This key step is often talked about, rather than precisely done. This will help you to manage the executive team, get them all on the same page, and imbue consistency and agreement on the proposed portfolio.

Chapter 3 is a review of the estimation techniques and methods. You are given possible models for use, from the Constructive Cost Model, to the Software Estimation Model, to the Software Lifecycle Model, and Function Point Analysis.

Chapter 4 takes things to the next level with highly mathematical, quantitative models and simulations. These "new" models will afford your organization with new possibilities. Warning: Be prepared to let the geek in you come out!

Chapter 5 walks you through the Canonical process model—capturing the stages in the workflow and roles, including the normal flow and exception events. This model helps you determine your ideal process model, including current state and process interactions.

Chapter 6 focuses on Calibration of your mode. It provides the ability to analyze resource, cost, and schedule impacts to provide a simulation of the optimal use of each throughout your projects.

Chapter 7 wraps things up with recommendations of how to actually put these tools and models into practice.

Whether you are a strategic executive or just beginning to understand the critical importance of such a Value Framework, these chapters will indeed serve to raise the bar with regard to possibilities not only for your organization, but also for your value-added contributions to how your organization will better align projects with strategic objectives to increase stakeholder engagement and create successful outcomes across the board.

Beth Ouellette
Managing Director, The Ouellette Group
Past President, Project Management
Institute New York City

Contents

Abstract

In this book, we propose a process for making rational choices in selection of strategic objectives as a quantitative as well as qualitative project management roadmap for the organization. The significant benefit of the process is that it helps bring about stakeholder alignment throughout the project. We will use case studies to illustrate the process in scenarios where significant disagreement initially existed between the stakeholders, for example, we will demonstrate the use of the methodology in aligning a strategic project portfolio selection process. The method used to create a dialog and agreement framework which enabled the participants to move forward beyond the initial log jam or misalignment. In this book we will:

- Develop a 'value framework' against which project choices can be evaluated;
- Rank objectives in the framework with key stakeholders using a modified Analytic Hierarchy Process. The resulting value framework objectives can be viewed as a basis for the grouping of investment tranches;
- Identify possible project portfolio selection options;
- Rank selection options against the value framework;
- Optimize the selections based on constrained resources (budget, staff, time) using a modified Efficient Frontier analysis technique;
- Optimize the execution using process simulations and to improve the accuracy of the estimation for future portfolio selection.

Keywords Project Management · IT Project Management · Software Estimation · Project Portfolio Management · Risk Management · Project Scheduling and Planning · Process Simulation Tools · Software Development · Process Modeling ICT

Chapter 1
Introduction

Introduction

According to the Standish group's eponymous Chaos reports, most organizations continue to struggle in delivering IT projects on time and within the budget. The process of estimating and planning work for the development of information technology (IT) projects continues to miss the mark with remarkable consistency which results in significant misuse of technology investments and resources (budget, people, time) and ultimately impacting the bottom line. The advent of information technology has changed its role from the backend data processing to business enabler. This puts a greater pressure on the success of projects. If a company had a more realistic understanding of the true costs of a project, would they invest their assets the same way or total cost of waste (TCW)? The field of project management has matured over the last few decades but many organizations are facing the same issues of under budget, over expectation, and failure of projects. Especially in an economic downtime, it is more critical to deliver projects on time, under budget, and show its return on investment (ROI). Today, it is more than simply showing the ROI, it is about how it has cut waste and make profit for the business. It is absolutely no question about how important project management is. Every year, billions dollars are wasted on mismanagement of projects. Can we do better? How do we lower the failure rate of projects? Are there missing opportunities out there as bad project planning squeezes out other projects? (Table 1.1).

The purpose of this book is to provide students, managers, and technologists methods to improve project success by improving three fundamental, but relatively unaddressed, areas of program and project management.

1. Help the organization quantify a strategic alignment between projects and organization direction.
2. Help the organization optimize a project portfolio based on the project risk (investment profile) and strategic value.
3. Help the organization perform agile project estimation based on a discrete event simulation of their process and feed that back into the strategic planning.

P. J. Morales and D. Anderson, *Process Simulation and Parametric Modeling for Strategic Project Management*, SpringerBriefs in Electrical and Computer Engineering, DOI: 10.1007/978-1-4614-6989-6_1, © The Author(s) 2013

Table 1.1 Chaos Summary for 2010. The Standish Group Inc. 2011

Standish report	% Successful	% Challenged	% Failed
1994	16	53	11
1996	27	33	40
1998	26	46	28
2000	28	49	23
2004	29	53	18
2006	35	46	19
2009	32	44	24

This book will offer CIOs, CTOs and IT Managers, IT Graduate Students an introduction to a set of technologies and methods that will help them understand how to better plan IT projects, manage risk and have better insight into the complexities of the IT development process. A novel methodology will be introduced that helps IT managers better plan and access risks in the early planning of a project cycle. By providing a better model for IT projects including early effort estimation, IT managers will be better equipped to make more effective project investment decisions. Moreover, the methodology will allow the IT manager to continually simulate scenarios throughout the lifecycle of the project and determine plausible alternatives before the risk becomes a reality. This allows the project managers to be agile as needed.

Projects are Investments

The reality of the state of project and portfolio management is that the manager is expected to deliver the project by the classic triple constraint criteria:

- On time
- On budget
- In scope and quality

Of course, it has to deliver the expected return on investment.

While these are reasonable objectives, there is another dimension which is often overlooked in project management and may be a larger cause of perceived project failure. This dimension is organizational alignment in selecting the project in the first place.

Let's look at an example analysis where we compare a portfolio of projects aligned to specific organizational goals. We will look at several techniques to ensure that the portfolio is

1. Aligned to the organizations objectives
2. Is constrained by a defined budget
3. Focused on aligning resources available for maximum returned value to the organization

We will demonstrate that, with a combination of techniques, even if one properly aligns projects with organizational objectives—the result can be less than optimal if initial estimates are off.

In order to develop a decision framework, an organization needs to develop a process for defining a quantitative mechanism for evaluating the relative merit of one project against another.

The process we propose here consists of the following steps:

1. Creating a value framework for categorizing selection success criteria.
2. Quantitatively ranking the relative merit of items in the value framework.
3. Identifying project choices to evaluate against the value framework.
4. Quantitatively ranking the project choices against the value framework.
5. Selecting an optimized solution set of project choices given constrained resources.

The intended result of this process is to develop a rational framework that incorporates a broad base of engagement for agreeing and selecting the priority of work for an organization as it goes through the project management life cycle.

We will explore the premise that traditional approaches to project management (PM) can benefit from better estimation practices in order for an organization to make better choices in its investments up front as well as better track progress of the project during execution. Broad parametric models are often 'tuned' to the organization for improved accuracy [43]. This approach has the effect of improving the overall utility of estimates for the organization as averaged over long periods of time. However, parametric models cannot account for a variety of conditions such as changes in staffing levels, changes in requirements that affect projects in real time and are therefore are limited with respect to the ultimate accuracy possible for an individual project [4, 7].

The process model proposed in later chapters uses individual estimates in a very different way. Rather than estimating an aggregate cost of the overall project, this model uses a process simulation to 'play forward' the implementation of each feature set over time based on project choices (staff availability, skill level, resources, etc.). This model also assumes that a certain amount of rework is inherent in all IT development work and so it is also factored into the work flow simulation. Other approaches deal with this in a hidden manner as part of their broad parametric formulas [8]. In traditional parametric models, rework is implicitly handled by averaging projects that include rework into the formulas. However, we show through our models later that the impact of the impact of even a small delay in a critical part of the IT implementation process can result in cascading effects. Hansman [26] studied the effects of delays in the air traffic control system and showed that small delays in one critical section of a system can have cascading and amplifying effects downstream causing far more damage than would be expected.

The result is that as you 'play forward' the simulation against specific choices made for that project, a projected cost and schedule can be derived in a way that other parametric modeling techniques account for only in an indirect way through averaging. In addition, as a project faces changes in scenarios and encounters surprises, these can be incorporated into the model and their effects in turn can be accounted for. The result is intended to provide more accurate results for a project as well as for the organization as a whole. This detailed approach of using granular parametric models combined with process analysis techniques has the added benefit of helping to simplify the basis formulas used in the models.

Chapter 2
Optimized Strategic Alignment

Collaborative Decision Framework

The process described here uses a quantitative approach to get alignment between multiple stakeholders who may not agree. In each of the Use Cases presented later, there was significant disagreement between the stakeholders. It should be noted that the process helped create a dialog and agreement framework which was based on value provided and constraints

1. Develop a 'value framework' against which project choices can be evaluated
2. Quantitatively rank objectives with key stakeholders
3. Use the value framework objectives as basis for investment tranches
4. Identify possible selection options
5. Quantitatively rank selection options against the value framework—therefore grouping into appropriate investment groups
6. Optimize selection based on constrained resources (budget, staff, time)

Analytic Hierarchy Process

A key component of the approach described here uses the Analytic Hierarchy Process. We will use a modified version to rank an alternative (choice) based on a set of criteria to ultimately achieve a goal.

AHP is often used process in Operations Research to facilitate decision making. There are a couple of known considerations when using the technique.

- Watch for inconsistent rankings. For example: A > B, B > C, therefore A > C (we will use a Python tool which will flag these inconsistencies)
- Adding additional alternatives can affect previous rankings (Fig. 2.1).

P. J. Morales and D. Anderson, *Process Simulation and Parametric Modeling for Strategic Project Management*, SpringerBriefs in Electrical and Computer Engineering, DOI: 10.1007/978-1-4614-6989-6_2, © The Author(s) 2013

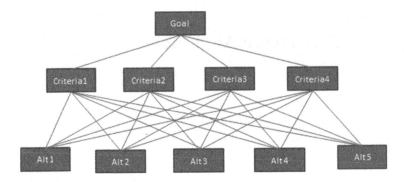

Fig. 2.1 Analytic Hierarchy Process

Analytic Hierarchy Process (Equations)

$$B = \begin{bmatrix} 1 & b_{12} & b_{13} & \cdots & \cdots & b_{1n} \\ \frac{1}{b_{12}} & 1 & b_{23} & \cdots & \cdots & b_{2n} \\ \frac{1}{b_{13}} & \frac{1}{b_{23}} & 1 & \cdots & \cdots & b_{3n} \\ \vdots & \vdots & \vdots & \vdots & \vdots & \vdots \\ \frac{1}{b_{1n}} & \frac{1}{b_{2n}} & \cdots & \cdots & \cdots & 1 \end{bmatrix}$$

Equation 2.1 – Basis Matrix

$$N = \begin{bmatrix} 1/n \sum_{i=1}^{n} b_{1i} & 1/n \sum_{i=1}^{n} b_{2i} & \cdots & 1/n \sum_{i=1}^{n} b_{ni} \end{bmatrix}$$

Equation 2.2 – Normalization vector

$$M = \begin{bmatrix} b_{11}/n_1 & b_{12}/n_2 & b_{13}/n_3 & \cdots & \cdots & b_{1n}/n_n \\ b_{21}/n_1 & b_{22}/n_2 & b_{23}/n_3 & \cdots & \cdots & b_{2n}/n_n \\ b_{31}/n_1 & b_{32}/n_2 & b_{33}/n_3 & \cdots & \cdots & b_{3n}/n_n \\ \vdots & \vdots & \vdots & \vdots & \vdots & \vdots \\ b_{n1}/n_1 & b_{n2}/n_2 & \cdots & \cdots & \cdots & b_{nn}/n_n \end{bmatrix}$$

Equation 2.3 – Normal Matrix

$$S = \begin{bmatrix} \sum_{i=1}^{n} m_{1n} \\ \sum_{i=1}^{n} m_{2n} \\ \vdots \\ \sum_{i=1}^{n} m_{nn} \end{bmatrix}$$

Equation 2.4 – Solution vector

$$S' = \begin{bmatrix} s_1 / \sum_{i=1}^{n} s_n \\ s_2 / \sum_{i=1}^{n} s_n \\ \vdots \\ s_n / \sum_{i=1}^{n} s_n \end{bmatrix}$$

Equation 2.5 – Normalized Solution vector

Identifying Organizational Objectives

In aligning projects with the goals of the organization we will use two techniques which help us identify the relative ranking of a set of corporate objectives. One might argue that a simple prioritized list might suffice but the techniques we will use here have two distinct advantages:

1. The list of objectives can be broadly vetted by key stakeholders in the organization
2. The resulting ordered list is aligned with the relative importance of that goal for the organization.

We begin by determining an organization's strategic priorities. Many organizations do this in a very organic manner or send out surveys to key executives. This is fine but how would we use this information to guide the choice of which projects need to be funded as part of the portfolio selection process without a quantitative ranking of value returned to the organization?

Let's look at a hypothetical example for an IT group in an organization. Let's begin with a possible list of potential strategic threads which the organization wants to use as its IT strategic drivers for the upcoming fiscal year:

1. Improve the external user experience.
2. Improve the internal user experience.
3. Improve the operational efficiency of the infrastructure.
4. Improve the operational efficiency of the applications.
5. Develop competitive differentiators.

Now, if you look at these objectives there are a number of problems. Let's assume that these are reasonable IT drivers. Let's also assume that we can describe them in a manner with sufficient detail that the organization can understand and support. How do we use these drivers as something we can translate into project portfolio selection criteria? A simple ranking of 1–5 for each driver can lead to a 5 way tie (I've seen it happen).

There are a couple of useful techniques used in portfolio management that can help us with this problem. The first technique is called Pairwise Analysis or Analytic Hierarchy Process. In short, the technique allows us to compare the relative importance of each factor to each other. For any two factors you define how important they are relative to each other:

- Factor A is much less important than Factor B
- Factor A is less important than Factor B
- Factor A is as important as Factor B
- Factor A is more important than Factor B
- Factor A is much more important than Factor B

If we do this for all the hypothetical factors we might end up with a matrix that looks something like this (Table 2.1):

If we assign a value for the range of importance where (Table 2.2).

We can then calculate a normalized relative ranking of each driver (Table 2.3):

We now know that "External User Experience" is the most important driver and it is about twice as important as the next driver "Internal User Experience"! The next two drivers are at least in the same range: "Internal User Experience" and "Competitive Differentiator"; followed by a distant last tie by the last two "Operational Efficiency" drivers. It is worth noting that this technique captures the "mood" of the organization at a point in time where the feeling is that improving the external or customer user experience seems to be the most important thing the company can do—by far.

This example is based on a real world survey for a company that was having some issues with perceived deficits in customer user experience. Is this a valid measure of the organizations drivers need to be? Is this a reasonable way to orchestrate a strategy? I would say—it depends. If they participants are thoughtful well intentioned managers who aren't reacting to emotional events then it may be a very good vehicle. There is a danger that creating this degree of quantification can lead people to believe that some deep hidden truth has been magically uncovered. The truth is that all we've done is created a way of seeing the mood of the participants in a different way. That can be valuable in its own right but one has to be careful to not be seduced into letting the process make a decision for you. It's just a visualization tool.

Table 2.1 Strategic factors

	External user experience	Internal user experience	Operational efficiency (infrastructure)	Operational efficiency (applications)	Competitive differentiator
Extenal user experience	Is as important as	Is more important than	Is much more important than	Is much more important than	Is much more important than
Internal user experience	Is less important than	Is as important as	Is more important than	Is more important than	Is more important than
Operatinal efficiency (infrastructure)	Is much less important than	Is less important than	Is as important as	Is as important as	Is less important than
Operatinal efficiency (applications)	Is much less important than	Is less important than	Is as important as	Is as important as	Is less important than
Competitive differentiator	Is less important than	Is less important than	Is more important than	Is more important than	Is as important as

Table 2.2 Strategic value conversion

Description	Value
Is extremely more important than	9.00
Is much more important than	6.00
Is more important than	3.00
Is as important as	1.00
Is less important than	0.30
Is much less important than	0.20
Is extremely less important than	0.10

Table 2.3 Strategic ranking

Rank	Ranked business drivers	Score (%)
1	External user experience	47.33
2	Internal user experience	24.21
3	Competitive differentiator	15.22
4	Operational efficiency (infrastructure)	6.62
5	Operational efficiency (applications)	6.62

Aligning Projects with Organizational Objectives

Now that we've identified our organization's objectives how do we get effort and resources to align with those strategic drivers? In this example we will select five projects, with their estimated cost, which may or may not align with our strategic drivers:

1. $730K Web site redesign
2. $425K Develop a disaster recovery infrastructure
3. $125K Develop a business process automation framework.
4. $250K Develop a data warehousing and reporting infrastructure
5. $260K Implement a data center automat

Now, without any basis on which projects to select the process often can best be described as an emotional arm wrestling match. I have seen stakeholders in organizations argue vehemently that if their project isn't done that we might as well shut our doors. Unfortunately, when the "squeaky wheel" gets the oil, the result is the other wheels soon begin squeaking! Pretty soon the squeaking is getting louder and louder.

How can we use the prioritized organizational drivers to help us sort things out? Can we measure the degree to which each project aligns to these drivers? Let's take a look at these five projects and calculate a hypothetical 'value' against each driver. Again, this is a subjective measure but at least we get a sense of which project gives us more lift in a particular direction (Tables 2.4, 2.5).

In this matrix we can determine the degree to which projects align with the strategic organizational drivers.

Table 2.4 Strategic portfolio alignment

	External user experience	Internal user experience	Operational effciency (infrastructure)	Operational effciency (appliations)	Competitive differentiator
Business process automation	Moderate	Extreme	Low	Strong	Moderate
Web site	Extreme	Strong	Low	Strong	Strong
Reporting infrastructure	Moderate	Strong	Low	Low	Moderate
Data center automation	Low	Moderate	Extreme	Strong	Low
Disaster recovery	Strong	Strong	Strong	Strong	Strong

Table 2.5 Ranking value conversion

Description	Value
Extreme	9
Strong	6
Moderate	3
Low	1
None	0
No rating	0

Table 2.6 Strategic portfolio ranking

Rank	Ranked project groups	Score (%)
1	Web site	30.28
2	Disaster recovery	25.63
3	Business process automation	19.30
4	Reporting infrastructure	14.78
5	Data center automation	10.01

If we diligently work our way through the matrix and decide how much alignment each project has with each driver and use the results to calculate a normalized ranking of the projects as follows (Table 2.6):

Looking at the results we see that overall the "Web Site" project provides the most overall lift against the strategic drivers followed by a Disaster Recovery project. Do these choices make sense? In fact, I was part of this selection process acting as the Chief Technologist in that organization and at the time I did believe that the Web Site was the most critical project for a lot of reasons—though most of them were perhaps more political. However, at that time I also felt that the next most important project would be the Data Center Automation project since my teams were dealing with a lot of frustration over our ability to respond in an agile manner to demand for infrastructure needs. So personal experience was influencing my choices rather than what was perhaps more important to the organization. There was also a coolness factor about using new technologies to solve problems in an innovative and cutting edge manner. A dynamically scalable Infrastructure As a Service (IaaS) model was personally very compelling. What the tool provides you is a lens through which you can see the organization's perspective of need. It would be easy to say: "I'm the person they hired to figure these things out. Why should I even consider the 'mood' of the organization." To some extent that is true but it is better to understand the need and even formalize a mandate which can be a powerful way to generate momentum.

Could we have gotten to a similar position intuitively? I actually don't think so. I think the advantage of a sort of dispassionate model like the one presented provides a framework that captures a broader sentiment of what the needs of the organization are. Clearly an improved Disaster Recovery project was critical but as a technologist I didn't have a lot of good options at the time. So my tendency was to be drawn to the fun projects that I had a strategy for and could make significant headway on. However, looking back at the model, I could see the organization's clear mandate to improve our Disaster Recovery capability and decided I needed to focus on that—even if it was less glamorous and harder to achieve.

Optimizing the Project Investment Portfolio

As we look at the possible projects we could invest in, we find that it might be possible to execute all of them if we have enough time and money to achieve the maximum possible strategic value (Table 2.7):

In this example, if we have a budget of $2,000,000 we find that all of the proposed projects can be achieved—assuming that we have enough time and resources (and that prerequisite technology staging is not an issue). What if we were had less resources? Is there a way we can optimize the strategic value for a different choice of projects (project portfolio). If we look at projects as an investment vehicle where for a given investment (or level of risk) we can achieve some maximum value. In the 1950s Harry Markowitz addressed this problem for traditional financial investments using a technique called Efficient Frontier analysis. It turns out that if you run through all the combinations of possible investments at any given level of risk, you end up with a maximum possible value return. The upper boundary of this risk/value curve is called the efficient frontier where you cannot possibly achieve more value (Fig. 2.2).

Table 2.7 Project budget selection

Project group	Strategic score (%)	Proposed cost
Business Process Automation	19.30	$730,000
Web Site	30.28	$425,000
Reporting Infrastructure	14.78	$125,000
Data Center Automation	10.01	$250,000
Disaster Recovery	25.63	$260,000
	Total cost	$1,790,000
	Constraint	$2,000,000
	Minimum score	100.00 %
	Solution cost	$1,790,000

Fig. 2.2 Efficient Frontier

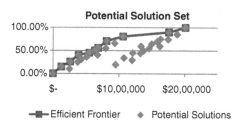

Fig. 2.3 Efficient Frontier
(underestimated cost)

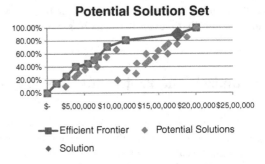

Now let's say we still have a budget of $2,000,000 but we estimated the cost of one of the projects as 30 % more than the iteration above. Now let's say the Web site redesign is now estimated at $949K.

(1) **$949K** Web site redesign
(2) $425K Develop a disaster recovery infrastructure
(3) $125K Develop a business process automation framework.
(4) $250K Develop a data warehousing and reporting infrastructure
(5) $260K Implement a data center automat

How would that affect our possible selection of projects out of the possible portfolio? (Fig. 2.3)

The resulting solution set based on an efficient frontier analysis would result in excluding the project that has the least strategic value for a given investment, in this case the Data Center Automation project (Table 2.8).

So, if we exclude project 4 (which has the lowest strategic value), we can meet our budget constraint but only achieve a maximum strategic value of approximately 90 %.

A ranked list of projects is important since we, as technologists, can often be swayed by personal, and perhaps subconcious factors such as affinity or knowledge of the technology involved, or perhaps a even a desire to learn something new (or perhaps even the desire to NOT have to learn something new). The point is we

Table 2.8 Strategic project selection (under estimated cost)

Project group	Strategic score (%)	Proposed cost
Business process automation	19.30	$949,000
Web site	30.28	$425,000
Reporting infrastructure	14.78	$125,000
Data center automation	10.01	$250,000
Disaster recovery	25.63	$260,000
	Total Cost	$2,009,000
	Constraint	2,000,000
	Minimum Score (%)	89.99
	Solution Cost	1,759,000

now have a perspective of how the projects theoretically align with the strategic values of the organization. However, we do have to keep in mind that these objectives need to be fluid as the needs of the organization can change radically based on even one single incident. One possible mechanism for doing this is a quarterly review of objectives.

It is important to note that the results of this prioritization exercise isn't a simple project execution list. It helps to understand the perceived priorities of key representatives of the organization but it should not be interpreted as an ordered list of projects. There are other factors that as a professional you would have to consider. As we will see in this chapter, another view has to be taken into account that can help you fit the prioritized drivers and projects into the longer term strategy. It may simply not be possible to execute projects in the ordered listed. There may be layers of other technology that would have to be implemented first in order to execute a project effectively. Bundling projects into larger programs in order to line up technology dependencies can lead to bundling more and more risk.

Rational Selection Process: Other Use Cases

It should be noted that the approach described above can be used in lots of situations where selecting an option based on a rational process can be of value. In the next example we used the process to help us sort through a technology selection. There were multiple groups involved and everyone had a preferred approach. After going through the process, a selection was made and even though the choice was different than a key stake holder wanted, the resulting option was selected unanimously (Tables 2.9, 2.10, 2.11, 2.12, 2.13 and 2.14).

Table 2.9 Use Case: Technology Selection, pair wise comparisons

	Cost control	Ease of implementation ramp up time	Ease of public cloud / private cloud inter operability	Support for DR / BC	Stability / robustness of end solution	Scalability	Ease of administration / maintenance / support
Cost control	is as important as	is much less important than	is much less important than	is much less important than	is much less important than	is much less important than	is much less important than
Ease of implementation ramp up time		is as important as	is as important as	is less important than	is much less important than	is less important than	is much less important than
Ease of public cloud / private cloud inter operability			is as important as	is much less important than	is much less important than	is much less important than	is much less important than
Support for DR / BC				is as important as	is as important as	is as important as	is less important than
Stability / robustness of end solution					is as important as	is more important than	is more important than
Scalability						is as important as	is less important than
Ease of administration / maintenance / support							is as important as

Table 2.10 Use Case: Technology Selection, hierarchical analysis

Technology Selection	Cost control	Ease of implementation ramp up time	Ease of public cloud / private cloud inter operability	Support for DR / BC	Stability / robustness of end solution	Scalability	Ease of administration / maintenance / support
Cost control	1	0.3	0.3	0.3	0.3	0.3	0.3
Ease of implementation ramp up time	6	1	1	0.6	0.3	0.6	0.3
Ease of public cloud / private cloud inter operability	6	1	1	0.3	0.3	0.3	0.3
Support for DR / BC	6	3	6	1	1	1	0.6
Stability / robustness of end solution	6	6	6	1	1	3	3
Scalability	6	3	6	1	0.6	1	0.6
Ease of administration / maintenance / support	6	6	6	3	0.6	3	1
	37	20.3	26.3	7.2	4.1	9.2	6.1

Normalized								Norm Sum	Norm %	Rank
Cost control	0.0270	0.0148	0.0114	0.0417	0.0732	0.0326	0.0492	0.2498	4%	7
Ease of implementation ramp up time	0.1622	0.0493	0.0380	0.0833	0.0732	0.0652	0.0492	0.5203	7%	5
Ease of public cloud / private cloud inter operability	0.1622	0.0493	0.0380	0.0417	0.0732	0.0326	0.0492	0.4461	6%	6
Support for DR / BC	0.1622	0.1478	0.2281	0.1389	0.2439	0.1087	0.0984	1.1279	16%	3
Stability / robustness of end solution	0.1622	0.2956	0.2281	0.1389	0.2439	0.3261	0.4918	1.8865	27%	1
Scalability	0.1622	0.1478	0.2281	0.1389	0.1463	0.1087	0.0984	1.0304	15%	4
Ease of administration / maintenance / support	0.1622	0.2956	0.2281	0.4167	0.1463	0.3261	0.1639	1.7389	25%	2

Table 2.11 Use Case: Technology Selection, strategic alignment of choices

Technology Selection	Cost control	Ease of implementation ramp up time	Ease of public cloud / private cloud inter operability	Support for DR / BC	Stability / robustness of end solution	Scalability	Ease of administration / maintenance / support
VM ESX	Moderate	Strong	Low	Moderate	Strong	Moderate	Strong
vCloud (Vcenter, vSphere, ESX)	Low	Moderate	Moderate	Moderate	Moderate	Moderate	Moderate
Xen	Strong	Strong	Low	Moderate	Moderate	Moderate	Moderate
KVM	Strong	Strong	Low	Moderate	Moderate	Moderate	Moderate
CloudStack/ VM Ware	Strong	Moderate	Moderate	Moderate	Moderate	Moderate	Moderate
CloudStack / Xen	Strong	Moderate	Moderate	Moderate	Moderate	Moderate	Moderate
CloudStack / KVM	Strong	Moderate	Moderate	Moderate	Moderate	Moderate	Moderate
RightScale	Moderate	Moderate	Strong	Strong	Moderate	Moderate	Moderate

Table 2.12 Use Case: Technology Selection, choice prioritization

Technology selection	Cost control	Ease of implementation ramp up time	Ease of public cloud / private cloud inter operability	Support for DR / BC	Stability / robustness of end solution	Scalability	Ease of administration / maintenance / support			
VM ESX	0.107	0.446	0.064	0.483	1.617	0.442	1.490	4.65	17.23%	1
vCloud (Vcenter, vSphere, ESX)	0.036	0.223	0.191	0.483	0.809	0.442	0.745	2.93	10.86%	5
Xen	0.214	0.446	0.064	0.483	0.809	0.442	0.745	3.20	11.87%	4
KVM	0.214	0.446	0.064	0.483	0.809	0.442	0.745	3.20	11.87%	4
CloudStack/ VM Ware	0.214	0.223	0.191	0.483	0.809	0.442	0.745	3.11	11.52%	3
CloudStack / Xen	0.214	0.223	0.191	0.483	0.809	0.442	0.745	3.11	11.52%	3
CloudStack / KVM	0.214	0.223	0.191	0.483	0.809	0.442	0.745	3.11	11.52%	3
RightScale	0.107	0.223	0.382	0.967	0.809	0.442	0.745	3.67	13.62%	2

Table 2.13 Use Case: Strategic Direction for a Tech Startup, pair wise comparisons

Tech Startup v2	Improve Operational Uptime	Improve End User Experience (UI)	Improve Development Efficiency	Improve Cost Management/Revenue Flow	Increase Market Depth/Reach	Improve Brand Awareness
Improve Operational Uptime	is as important as	is more important than	is more important than	is as important as	is more important than	is much more important than
Improve End User Experience (UI)		is as important as	is more important than	is less important than	is less important than	is as important as
Improve Development Efficiency			is as important as	is less important than	is less important than	is more important than
Improve Cost Management/Revenue Flow				is as important as	is more important than	is more important than
Increase Market Depth/Reach					is as important as	is as important as
Improve Brand Awareness						is as important as

Table 2.14 Use Case: Strategic Direction for a Tech Startup, hierarchical analysis

Tech Startup v2	Improve Operational Uptime	Improve End User Experience (UI)	Improve Development Efficiency	Improve Cost Management /Revenue Flow	Increase Market Depth /Reach	Improve Brand Awareness			
Improve Operational Uptime	1	3	3	1	3	6			
Improve End User Experience (UI)	0.6	1	3	0.6	0.6	1			
Improve Development Efficiency	0.6	0.6	1	0.6	0.6	3			
Improve Cost Management/Revenue Flow	1	3	3	1	3	3			
Increase Market Depth/Reach	0.6	3	3	0.6	1	1			
Improve Brand Awareness	0.3	1	0.6	0.6	1	1			
	4.1	11.6	13.6	4.4	9.2	15			
Improve Operational Uptime	0.244	0.259	0.221	0.227	0.326	0.400	1.676	27.9%	1
Improve End User Experience (UI)	0.146	0.086	0.221	0.136	0.065	0.067	0.721	12.0%	4
Improve Development Efficiency	0.146	0.052	0.074	0.136	0.065	0.200	0.673	11.2%	5
Improve Cost Management/Revenue Flow	0.244	0.259	0.221	0.227	0.326	0.200	1.476	24.6%	2
Increase Market Depth/Reach	0.146	0.259	0.221	0.136	0.109	0.067	0.937	15.6%	3
Improve Brand Awareness	0.073	0.086	0.044	0.136	0.109	0.067	0.515	8.6%	6

Chapter 3
Improving the Process

In the previous chapters we discussed three very important objectives:

1. Identifying organizational objectives which the IT organization can align with.
2. Aligning project choices with the objectives.
3. Optimizing the choices of projects to maximize value to the organization.

While these objectives are valuable and worthy of effort on their own merit; there is one problem. The effectiveness of the objectives above is limited by the accuracy of the estimation of cost. In most organizations this is addressed either not at all, or through the use of broad band estimation models such as COCOMO or SLIM. While these models have been around for many years, they have several issues:

1. They primarily deal with software development projects.
2. Their estimation is based on a statistical aggregation of many projects—not of the specifics for the projects at hand.
3. The models are not responsive to changes in the project environment.
4. They do not provide a measure which tells you how resilient the estimation is to change.

Review of Traditional Estimation Methods

An early attempt formalize IT project cost estimation is the Wideband Delphi approach to developed by the Rand Corporation in 1948 and refined by Barry Boehm during his tenure at Rand in the 1970s [51]. This process is still used today in many corporations.

In 1981, Barry Boehm developed one of the most successful and widely used parametric estimation models: COCOMO (Constructive Cost Model) which has been used by a large number of commercial and military projects [7]. In this landmark work, Boehm proposed an approach to performing IT cost estimates as an engineering problem.

P. J. Morales and D. Anderson, *Process Simulation and Parametric Modeling for Strategic Project Management*, SpringerBriefs in Electrical and Computer Engineering, DOI: 10.1007/978-1-4614-6989-6_3, © The Author(s) 2013

The initial COCOMO Model had three different forms based on the following formula:

$$E = a(KSLOC)^b$$

Equation 3.1—Basic COCOMO formula

where:

KSLOC—one thousand lines of code
E—estimated effort (e.g. in person-months)
a—complexity factor
b—scaling exponent (usually close to 1)

A major approach for estimation of effort and duration is COCOMO. This approach was explored for the case study project but unfortunately, as we will see, a fundamental obstacle involved estimating the end count of lines of code for the project.

In 1997, Barry Boehm released a major revision with COCOMO II. Significant changes include modifications to the parameter b according to the following cost factors [8]:

- Precedentedness, or how familiar is the domain for which the system being developed
- Development flexibility, how rigorous versus flexible is the development process
- Architecture or risk resolution, how much risk is involved in the architecture for the system being developed
- Team cohesion, how difficult are the team interactions
- Process maturity, how mature is the developing organization, now based on a SEI CMM Maturity level.

COCOMO II uses a 3 level model that supports increasingly detailed estimates throughout the evolution of a project:

Early prototyping level: simple formula is used for effort estimation

$$PM = (NOP \times (1 - \%reuse/100))/PROD$$

Equation 3.2—COCOMO prototyping effort

where

PM is the effort in person-months,
NOP is the number of object points and PROD is the productivity ranging from very low: 7 to high: 50)
Where Object Points is a methodology for calculating product size now incorporated into COCOMO II.
Productivity is a throughput measure of ability to produce a given amount of product (e.g. lines of code) in a given amount of time.

Early design level:

$$PM = A \times Size^B \times M + PM_m$$

Equation 3.3—COCOMO(early design)

where

$$M = PERS \times RCPX \times RUSE \times PDIF \times PREX \times FCIL \times SCED$$
$$PM_m = (ASLOC \times (AT/100))/ATPROD$$

A = 2.5 initially,

Size is the estimated product size in KSLOC,

B varies from 1.1 to 1.24 depending on novelty of the project, development flexibility, risk management approaches and the process maturity.

Post-architecture level: Estimates based on lines of source code and design artifacts.

In 1974, Dr. Randall Jensen and colleagues [29] working at the Huges Corporation, began working on the problem of IT project estimation. The "Jensen Model" was an early attempt to capture an algorithmic approach to developing effort and duration estimates for IT system development from estimated product size as well as many other characteristics of the project. The "Jensen Model" evolved into what is now known as the SEER-Software Estimation Model (SEM) [21]. The term SEER is based on the verb to see. The SEER model, as it is now commonly referred, continues to exist as a commercial product under the Golorath Corporation [30].

In 1978, Larry Putnam (a retired US Army Colonel), developed the SLIM (Software Lifecycle Model) methodology. SLIM's parametric modeling basis formulas are similar to COCOMO's. In 1982 SLIM was released for the new IBM PC platform. SLIM's parametric models incorporate a Rayleigh distribution for estimates of project effort, schedule and defects [43]. The Rayleigh distribution is a common choice for stochastic process(es) which have a relatively fast ramp up but a longer tail. This models the initiation of a process and the gradual completion of work in expending effort. Less complex items which require less effort will complete more quickly whereas more complex items may take proportionally more time (Fig. 3.1).

This model assumes that staffing peaks at $t = t_d$. In the real world, especially one where staff may work on more than one project, staffing levels may not be as predictable or controllable and may not quite fit a Rayleigh distribution. (The model in this study addresses this problem—more on that later.) SLIM, models effort utilization in a project by defining a productivity (P) as the ratio of software product Size (S) and the effort required to produce it (E) or P = S/E. The full form of the SLIM equation (solved for effort by Huang) [31] is shown below:

$$E = \left((LOC)B^{0.333}/P^3\right)\left(1/t^4\right)$$

Equation 3.4—SLIM Effort Formula

Fig. 3.1 Rayleigh distribution

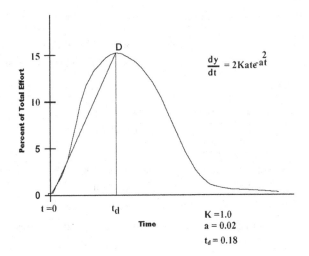

$$\frac{dy}{dt} = 2Kate^{-at^2}$$

K = 1.0
a = 0.02
t_d = 0.18

where

E—effort in person-months
LOC—lines of code
T—project duration in months
B—special skill factor ranging from 0.16 to 0.39
P—productivity parameter that reflects:

management practices
software development practices used (standards, training)
programming language used
software environment
(e.g. tools, automation, documentation, training)
skill and experience of the development team complexity of the application

Function Point Analysis, Developed by Capers Jones [50], which has a proprietary database of over 8000 projects. It uses Function Points [50] as input of product size in order to derive effort and schedule, resources, deliverables and cost estimates. It offers 4 levels of granularity including:

- Project
- Phase
- Activity
- Task

Function Point estimation is an attempt to estimate product size independent from counting lines of code.

A Function Point is derived from Table 3.1.

Table 3.1 Function point inputs

Inputs	Sets of data supplied by users or other program
Outputs	Sets of data produced for users or other programs
Inquiries	Means for users to interrogate the system
Data files	Collections of records which the system modifies
Interfaces	Files/databases shared with other systems

Each of these factors are weighted by a complexity factor of Low, Average or High to compute an Unadjusted Function Point (UFP):

$$UFP = \sum_{i=1}^{5} \sum_{j=1}^{3} w_{ij} z_{ij}$$

Equation 3.5—Unadjusted function point calculation

where, z_{ij} is the count for component I at complexity j and w_{ij} is the fixed weight assigned to each factor.

Estimates are often over ruled or ignored by organizations that are convinced the project needs to be done by a certain date "no matter what". However, without an engineering basis, opinions dominate (some opinions dominate more than others). Perhaps one of the parametric modeling approaches strongest contributions to IT project cost estimation is that it provides an engineering basis which makes opinion driven decision making more difficult.

Chapter 4
An Introduction to Quantitative Process Simulation

As we've seen so far, one of the key elements to selecting an optimized program portfolio that achieves the best strategic value for the organization is being able to estimate effectively. Unfortunately this is an area that can benefit from better tools and processes. In order to improve our ability to estimate we need more responsive tools. In this chapter, we will demonstrate how projects diverge from original estimates in a myriad of ways that are often unpredictable at the beginning. The amount of 'learning' that is part of the process of defining and building a system can be a huge source of underestimation. We will use a quantitative computational parametric modeling technique to demonstrate how even well planned projects can get off track quickly.

In this chapter we will look at a new method for improving the estimation of cost for IT projects in an organization. This model will improve on previous estimation techniques in the following ways

1. Create a model that can be used by project managers early in the estimation process.
2. Provide tuning parameters that can account for the specifics of the project environment.
3. Provide a method that can handle more than just software development projects.
4. Provide a measure of how resilient a particular approach to a project is when dealing with changes in the project environment.
5. Provide a method for understanding the impact changes in real time for the project environment.

The detailed parametric model developed here can be used for initial estimates of project effort and duration. Later we will demonstrate how the model can be used to account for real world scenarios such as:

New requirements
Changed requirements
Constrained staffing availability
Staffing changes.

P. J. Morales and D. Anderson, *Process Simulation and Parametric Modeling for Strategic Project Management*, SpringerBriefs in Electrical and Computer Engineering, DOI: 10.1007/978-1-4614-6989-6_4, © The Author(s) 2013

Modeling Objectives: Purpose, Complexity and Fidelity

When we endeavor to model our perception of the real world, questions naturally arise. How rich should the model be; how realistic? What do we include in the model and what can we exclude? We can agree that models are simplified articulations of realistic phenomena as perceived through our senses. It can be argued that we can never truly capture a 'complete' reality in a model. The model is always by definition a filtered view of the universe articulated with the limitations of the language used.

A simple thought experiment can demonstrate the inherent limitations of models. Suppose we want to model a simple physical artifact. We could go around the room and ask each of us to articulate some aspect of an object, say a pencil. We could in fact continue articulating information on a simple object for a very long time (perhaps forever—but that is outside the scope of this study). So if we cannot hope to model the world in a complete and realistic manner then are models of any value?

Fast and Frugal Heuristics

Fast and Frugal heuristics as proposed by Malcom [23] and Gigernzer [25] provide some guidance on how to model effectively. The model developed here uses principles of Fast and Frugal Heuristics as a guide.

Fast and Frugal Heuristics propose that a model should hold true to two principles:

1. The model should be bounded in its purpose.
2. The model should be 'ecological' or not violate the fidelity of the scope it is modeling.

First, the model should be "bounded" in its purpose. This is in contrast to a Bayesian view of the world where the expected outcome of some event can be predicted on the known probabilities of all expected outcomes (which can become monumentally expensive to calculate). Fast and Frugal Heuristics take an aggressive approach to limiting the dimensions of the model. In the case of the detailed parametric model proposed here, the purpose of the modeling is to accurately estimate the duration, effort and cost of building an IT system.

Second, the model should be "consistent". That is, the limited set of rules in the model should not contradict reality. Within its narrow confines, the model should reflect the real world with a reasonable degree of fidelity. In the case of our detailed parametric model, changing requirements and variations in resource availability should not invalidate the model.

Several technologies were investigated for our modeling. From the beginning we decided that a broad parametric approach would not be responsive enough.

This is especially true of day to day changes in the system development project being modeled. Broad parametric models tend to define gross patterns such as: "how is the forest doing this year against a general long term trend. The daily process of how the trees are doing as part of this long term general trend are not typically modeled together. In fact, the two are very closely related. The general long trend is an outcome of how the more granular short term processes are doing. It is just very difficult to develop models which can address both aspects in a holistic way.

Modeling Approach

The modeling approach selected here is the System Dynamics approach developed by Jay Forrester at MIT. The approach combines the ability to define granular parametric models integrated into a set of tools that facilitates the definition of process behaviors using gadgets to connect a series of discrete behaviors into a more complex model.

The general process for developing the model consists of:

Step 1   Capturing detailed data for the granular execution of a defined and consistent process. That is not to say that there aren't bugs or mistakes but you need detailed time and effort data for at least one full project cycle.

Step 2   Developing a process model. The models used in this book were developed in Python with Excel acting as the user interface for configuration data as well the repository for result data.

Step 3   Calibrating the model. Much of the effort in the development of the models was spent calibrating the parametric 'transfer' functions which model the amount of time spent in each stage based on the size and complexity of the work being processed.

Using simulation tools developed in the Python, one can build a model that combines aspects of queuing theory, workflow simulation, combined with granular parametric behaviors. While the parametric models defined by Boehm and Putnam clearly indicate there is a non-linear relationship between the time required to implement a feature and its complexity, we will further show using the models presented here that:

- The effect of not having enough resources to provide the amount of effort required to complete an activity results in longer than expected delays, even if we take the non-linear relationship between size/complexity to effort required.
- The delays are further compounded downstream in the process where there is an inefficient use of resources even if there are more resources available than resources required to perform activities which are not yet ready.
- Once the delayed activity is completed the imbalance continues to create delays as backlogged work in process (wip) is queued.

Parametric Modeling with a Workflow Process Simulation

The model developed here represents a very granular and detailed parametric modeling approach to project estimation which uses simple parametric models within a process simulation. While it uses a central 'basis' parametric equation based on one of five leading estimation models, the 'estimate' is calculated for a subset of the project (e.g. user story, feature request thread, change request etc.) and a process mechanism is employed to 'play forward' the implementation. This approach has the advantage of separating the problem into two parts. Using a simpler form of a traditional parametric equation we can model a basic relationship between the product and the effort and time required to produce it. This simpler parametric model is used in a process simulation model which can account for issues which affect the implementation directly (changes in resource availability, new requirements etc.).

A Network Model of Linked Stages of Work

We propose that any process, can be represented by a linked network of stages of work. Each of these stages represents one step in the larger system where the time it takes to complete the stage depends on (Fig. 4.1):

1. The amount of effort required to process the inbound work-in-process.
2. The amount of effort available to complete the work.

Differences between the local resources required and the local resources available determine the time it takes to pass through the work-in-process. The relationship between effort required is non-linear based on gross size and complexity.

So based on these relationships we can see that several workflow disruptors can occur:

1. A large or complex inbound work item can cause other incoming work to begin to queue.
2. A reduction is resources—even a temporary one—can cause the incoming work to begin to queue

Queuing, Bottlenecks and Other Stochastic Behaviors

As work queues, there are cascading downstream effects which multiply the impact of the delay. First, other downstream stages of work begin to 'starve'. That is,

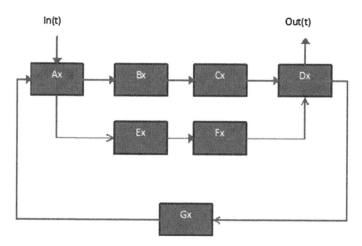

Fig. 4.1 Hypothetical process flow

resources may be available to do the work but since no work is reaching them (other than any already queued work-in-process) then the resources would remain idle.

As work begins to flow downstream, additional queuing will begin to occur as the backlog of work now starts to reach these stages. The result is a sort of 'non-laminar' flow of work from stage to stage—creating inefficiencies in resource utilization in each of the stages.

Chapter 5
Developing a Canonical Process Model

What is the Ideal Process

What do we mean by the 'Canonical Process Model'? This is the officially defined model of the process which describes the stages in the workflow, the roles, and how work flows normally and in the event of an exception. We make a distinction between the defined process and the actual process being executed 'on-the-ground'. Very often, even if there is a process well defined, the actual process will begin to stray for a number of reasons:

1. Lack of proper initial training results in ad-hoc behavior.
2. Lack of refresh training may cause confusion and result in ad-hoc behavior.
3. People may find ways to alter the process either to improve or shorten steps but it is not captured and maintained in the Canonical Model.
4. Exceptions not captured in the process may be handled in extraneous ways.
5. The process may have changed but the workflow has remained the same.

Capturing the 'As Is' Process

Very often it is advantageous to find ways to understand the actual process being followed. The most common ways to capture the process are:

1. Surveys of participants
2. Interviews

Unfortunately, both of these processes are flawed. In the case of surveys, the actual design of the survey can lead to incorrect data. In the case of interviews, people may not want to admit they aren't following the defined process—even though they may not believe it is a good design.

P. J. Morales and D. Anderson, *Process Simulation and Parametric Modeling for Strategic Project Management*, SpringerBriefs in Electrical and Computer Engineering, DOI: 10.1007/978-1-4614-6989-6_5, © The Author(s) 2013

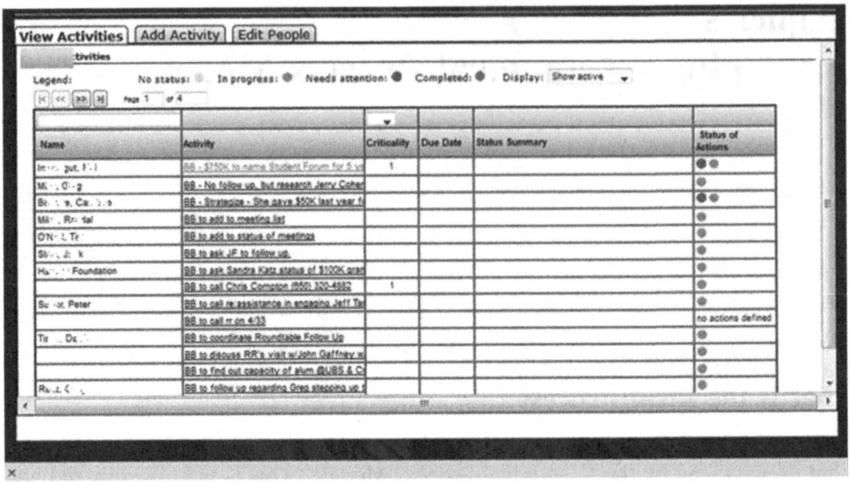

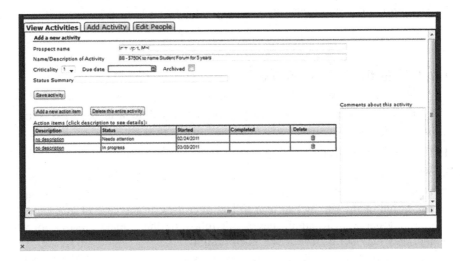

Fig. 5.1 Process facilitation tool (dashboard). Example of an activity dashboard showing all work-in-progress

Therefore, the results of both of these approaches is suspect. Is there a way to capture the process without skewing the results. We propose that there is! Ideally, if you can facilitate the process interactions by creating a hybrid ticketing/e-mail notification system where each request for work is entered into a system with the following information:

Fig. 5.2 Example of spawned activities for a task

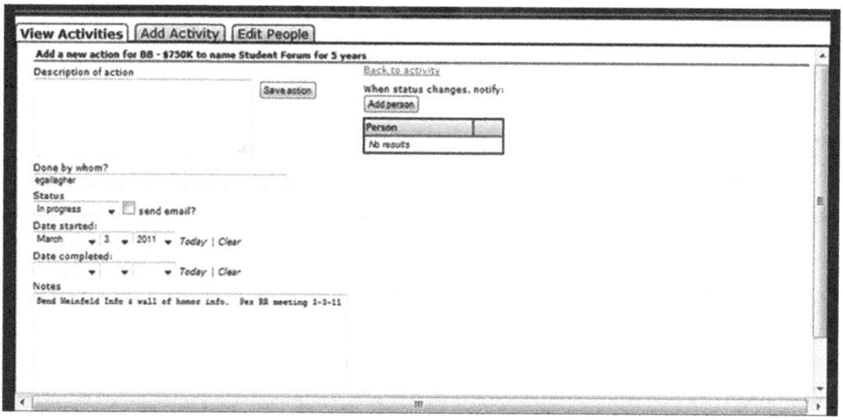

Fig. 5.3 Example of the application capturing the details of an activity

1. Requestor name
2. Estimated effort
3. Estimated due date
4. Criticality

Capturing Process Interactions

Here is an example of an application that was used to capture the interactions in a project. This particular application was designed to run on an Android tablet but we make no arguments that it needs to be tablet based. However, if you can get the team to interact—or to create mini contracts with each other—and capture the progression of work through states capturing:

1. Estimated duration
2. Estimated effort
3. Actual duration
4. Actual effort
5. Timing of state transitions

Then we can display the process interactions on a network diagram where the nodes represent states in the process.

The advantage of capturing process this way is that these are real interactions used to get the work done; whereas interviews and surveys are abstract at best (Figs. 5.1, 5.2, 5.3).

Chapter 6
Quantitative Process Simulation

The objective of using a quantitative process simulation model is to:

- Provide the ability to analyze the impact of resource allocation on cost and schedule
- Demonstrate the effect of resource timing on cost and schedule
- Separate factors for skill and process for each stage in the development of an iterative project
- Demonstrate the complex integration of multiple teams participating in the system development project.

Ultimately, effective use of resources in an organization depends greatly on the ability to understand the process. Process involves many factors including people, technology and methodology. It is difficult to account for very specific contributions and interactions among these factors using gross statistical modeling approaches. As we've discussed earlier, the approach used here is intended to provide a mechanism for providing a better estimation method in order to allow you to accomplish objectives in a more consistent manner and therefore help you use resources more effectively.

The models also take into account that there can be significant differences in a team's dynamic due to very human factors including:

- Team chemistry
- Degree of familiarity with each other and facility to communicate
- Leadership.

These aspects can be accounted for in as granular manner as desired using this modeling approach. However, measuring them is another matter. The basis for this model is to approximate the behavior of an IT development project by simulating a workflow process. In this case the process was modeled using a modified version of the Unified Process used in a real life Case Study Project we will refer to as P1.

P. J. Morales and D. Anderson, *Process Simulation and Parametric Modeling*
for Strategic Project Management, SpringerBriefs in Electrical and Computer
Engineering, DOI: 10.1007/978-1-4614-6989-6_6, © The Author(s) 2013

Model Calibration

The transport latency through any part of the process is governed by medium grained exponential transfer functions. Unfortunately, tuning the model proved tricky as adjustments in one process affected the entire system. The principal objective is to calibrate the factors for the polynomial that governs the pass through time for each node. The general form of the equation looks something like this:

$$E = M^{(A * S/10)} + M * B + C$$

Equation 6.1—Model Workflow Throughput formula

where

E = Effort
M = Element magnitude
A = Element Complexity exponential factor
B = Element Complexity linear factor
S = Resource skill factor (capability 1–10)
C = Scalar adjustment.

After hundreds of hours tuning the model, we were able to stabilize the complex interaction between the fine grained parametric formulas and the flow of work from process to process. The local balance between minimum resources required versus resources available determine the amount of time it takes to process the work.

We used data gathered in the case study project described in the appendix to tune the model parameters. In the end, the best method in tuning the model was by successive approximations. Here are the factors we derived from tuning the models (Tables 6.1, 6.2, 6.3, 6.4 and 6.5):

Note that in this case we defined a project team member with a Skill Factor of 8 (on a scale of 1–10) as a good fit for the project but also a nominal measure for the model. We will demonstrate that using this model, once calibrated, that it is possible to use very localized balancing of resources available against resources

Table 6.1 Model analysis factors

Analysis factors	
A	2.4
B	2.2
C	2.1

Table 6.2 Model design factors

Design factors	
A	2.7
B	2.5
C	2.0

Table 6.3 Model coding factors	Coding factors	
	A	2.5
	B	2.5
	C	2.1

Table 6.4 Model test design factors	Test design factors	
	A	2.1
	B	2.1
	C	2.1

Table 6.5 Model testing and integration factors	Testing and integration factors	
	A	2.1
	B	2.1
	C	2.1

required, that it is possible to determine an optimal resource load to complete the project in a minimum scheduled time. Even if you add more resources than required, at a given point in time, that you will not reduce the schedule.

Baseline Configuration

The first data run was executed with essentially no resource constraints. The effort available was set at significantly greater than effort required in all five sub-processes. That is, each process was assigned approximately 7 resources for the duration of the project. For the baseline run, the re-work component of the model was turned off (Fig. 6.1).

The Case Study Project estimate was based on a Use Case Points method. This resulted in effort estimates for each component of work in the implementation of the system. Use Case points do not however address estimation of calendar time as that depends on the configuration of the team.

Presented above are the results of the first data run after calibration. Minimum effort and durations are used since a project manager could arbitrarily budget for and assign a much larger team than needed. As we have seen in the first order model, at some point, there are diminishing returns as one adds team members. This parallels real life where work cannot be atomically divided beyond some logical limit.

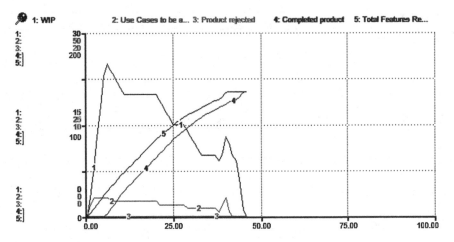

Fig. 6.1 Process model results—baseline configuration

Resource Optimization

In this run, resources were aligned with the effort demand predicted by the model. Here we plan to have just enough resources to keep up with the effort demand but not so much that there was a lot of slack (Fig. 6.2).

It should also be noted that the balance between minimum effort required and effort available needn't be perfect. In several instances, more effort was required than was available as can be seen early in the Analysis graph. The system stabilized as long as this imbalance was brief and there was enough slack in the following weeks to absorb the imbalance. The flow of work from phase to phase stayed laminar. We will explore these limits in more detail in sections to follow.

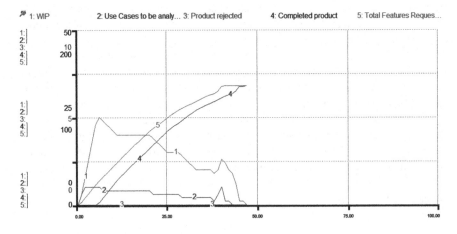

Fig. 6.2 Process model results—resource optimization run

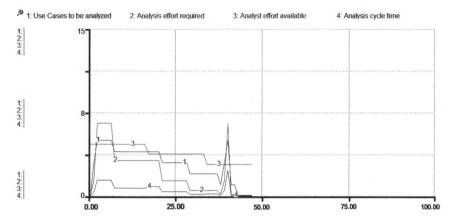

Fig. 6.3 Process model results—resource optimized scenario analysis view

In the Fig. 6.3 we see that in the Analysis phase of the project the model predicts the following:

- We set the resources available to generally be more than the resources required for the duration of the project. (Effort required is the amber line—marked 2 in the graph).
- The model shows the number of analysis resources required to be much heavier up front in the earlier weeks of the project; there is a quick ramp up in resources required in the first 5 weeks of the project,
- Analysis Resources Required drop off sharply from a peak of approximately 7 analysts in the first few weeks to about 4 after the 4th week; Analysis Resources Required dramatically drops off again after week 18 to approximately 2 resources
- There is another small spike in analysis resources required in the last few weeks with the project ending in week 47 (defined as 0 items of Work in Process—WIP across any of the processes).
- While Resources Available is generally above the Resources Required, there are a couple of instances where Resources Required exceeds Resources Available. The model was able absorb the imbalance since this is a short lived imbalance (<4 weeks) AND there is a surplus of Resources Required in the following weeks.
- In general, this pattern follows typical Unified Process resource utilization. Heavier Analysis at the beginning of the project diminishing as the project goes on.
- The Available Resources is shown in the graph as a pink marked as 3 in the graph. You will notice that in the beginning we chose a steady number of resources starting at 5 from weeks 0–16, then we dropped the number of resources to 4 from week 16–32 and then down to 3 till week 47.
- As noted earlier, Analysis Resources Required exceeded Analysis Resources Available for short periods of time which did not appear to have delayed the project. The flow of work through this phase was 'laminar' in the sense that there were no flow disturbances through this phase.

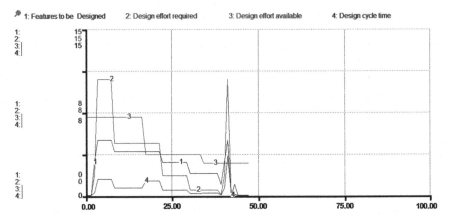

Fig. 6.4 Resource optimized scenario—design view

The Fig. 6.4 depicts the flow of work through the Design process. Similar to the Analysis phase, Design Resources Available are generally more than Design Resources Required with only short periods where the imbalance shifts. As we will see later as we perform some sensitivity analysis of the mode, these short lived imbalances are absorbed if the durations is mall and the difference isn't excessive.

In these models a critical measure of the balance between Resources Required versus Resources Available is a measure we call Cycle Time. Cycle Time is calculated by dividing Resources Required by Resources Available. When they are in balance, the results are lower stable Cycle Time.

We can see from the Figs. 6.5, 6.6 and 6.7, Coding, Test Design and Testing are similarly stable.

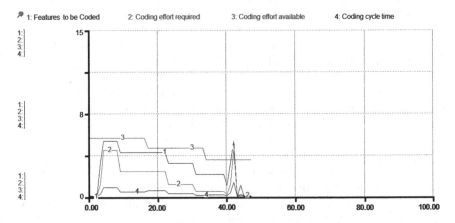

Fig. 6.5 Process model results—resource optimized scenario coding view

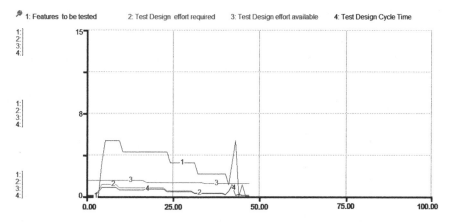

Fig. 6.6 Process model results—resource optimized scenario test design view

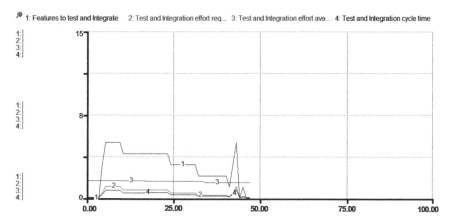

Fig. 6.7 Process model results—resource optimized scenario testing and integration view

Sensitivity Analysis: Early Constraint Scenario

In the previous examples the model was able to predict the optimal level of effort and schedule based on an order of magnitude estimate of Use Case complexity for 41 Use Cases (Fig. 6.8).

Now, what if the resource constraint was a relatively small one but it happened at a critical point in the project life cycle. What would those results look like? This example illustrates a small dip in early resource availability at the beginning of the project, similar to a delay in finding a suitable resource to work on requirements early in the project. In this case, this early delay caused the project to complete in 56 weeks—versus 47 weeks in the Resource Optimized model above.

In this run, we purposely limited Analysis Resources Available to 1 resource available for the first 5 weeks ramping up to 3 resources available for 5–10 weeks

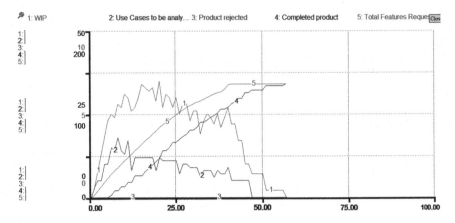

Fig. 6.8 Process model results—early resource constraint scenario

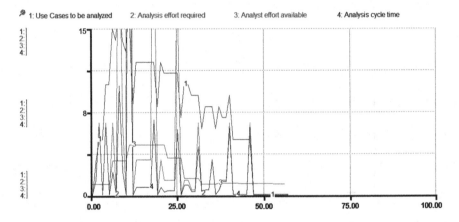

Fig. 6.9 Process model results—resource constraint scenario, analysis view

(the pink line marked as 3 on the graph). There are some interesting observations (Fig. 6.9):

- Analysis Cycle Time (the green line marked as 4 on the graph) rises sharply as Analysis Resources Available (the pink line marked as 3 on the graph) falls far below Analysis Resources Required (the amber line marked as 2 on the graph) during the first 4 weeks.
- The number of Use Cases to be Analyzed (the blue line marked as 1 on the graph) increases during the first several weeks of the project as work starts to queue.
- Even though there are sufficient Design Resources Available at the beginning of the project, there are cascading effects observable as a result of the imbalance in the preceding Analysis stage of work.
- As work starts to flow into Design sporadically from Analysis (due to the deficit of resources available in the Analysis stage) there is a cascading effect

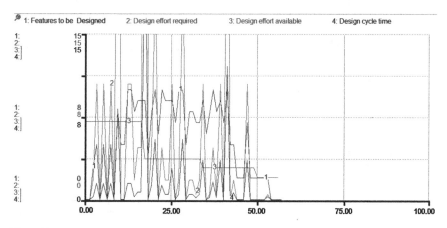

Fig. 6.10 Process model results—early resource constraint scenario, design view

observable of spikes and valleys of Design Resources Required. During this
time Design resources would not be utilized effectively (Fig. 6.10).

- As a result there are some very high spikes in Design Cycle Time starting at
  around week 15. Delays in the Analysis phase are now being reflected as work
  arriving late for coding and resources which were earlier available for coding
  not being used efficiently.
- Also as Design resources start to ramp down based on the previously planned
  flow of work, there is an imbalance of Design Resources Required to Design
  Resources available leading to the very significant Design Cycle Time spikes.
- The effects of delays and resulting spikes of cycle time required begin to get
  absorbed in the Coding stage. There are still some significant spikes of Coding
  Effort Required, especially at week 12 and week 23 but they seem to settle after
  week 30 (Fig. 6.11).

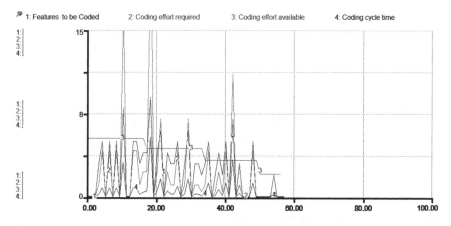

Fig. 6.11 Process Model results—early resource constraint scenario, coding view

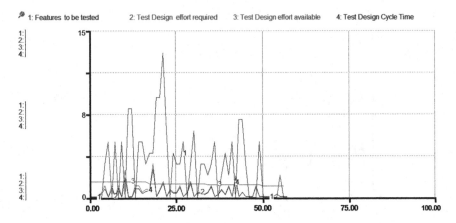

Fig. 6.12 Process model results—early resource constraint scenario, test design view

- The pathological pattern of spiky cycles of effort supply and demand continue through the end of the project (week 56). Anecdotal observations of projects in stress do seem to follow this pattern as there are high activity responses to delays in previous stages of a process,
- In general, Coding Effort Available is generally above the Coding Effort required. One might ask, what would happen if there was an additional resource anomaly in this or any other stage of the project. In all likelihood the results would be far more impactful.
- The pathological 'spikyness' in work flow continues through the project for Test Design but to a far less extent.
- Generally Test Design Resources Available are above Test Design Resources Required. As a result, it is unlikely that Test Design contributes any significant delay to the project (Fig. 6.12).
- The 'spikyness' continues through Testing and Integration (Fig. 6.13).
- Again, there is a relatively even balance between Resources Required and Resources Available.

Sensitivity Analysis: Serious Delays

In this scenario, resources were heavily constrained such that each process only had 2 resources assigned for the duration of the project. As a result, the project completes in 79 weeks!

Interestingly, the resource constraint early in the sub-processes cascade downstream and create their own workflow perturbations. In the first run where there were no resource constraints, the work flow from sub-process to sub-process was fairly laminar. As work flowed into a process, there were sufficient resources

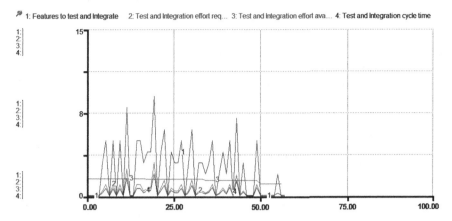

Fig. 6.13 Process model results—early resource constraint scenario, testing and integration view

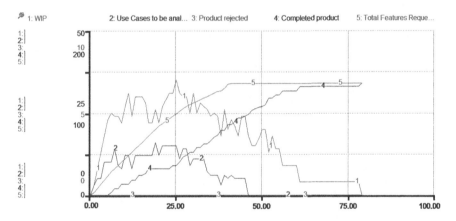

Fig. 6.14 Process model results—highly resource constraint scenario

to handle it. In contrast, the workflow in the resource constrained model resulted in more chaotic transitions of work downstream (Fig. 6.14).

In the real world this translates into the effect where not having enough Requirement Analysts results in work going into design in a start stop fashion. One week a developer may not have any code to implement, the following week there might be an overload and so on. The effects of this kind of non-laminar workflow are highly disruptive and cause significant inefficiencies. It can also translate into poor quality product as team members are pushed to catch up (Figs. 6.15, 6.16, 6.17, 6.18 and 6.19).

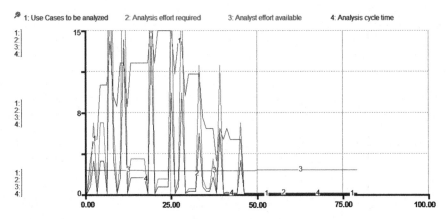

Fig. 6.15 Process model results—highly resource constrained scenario, analysis view

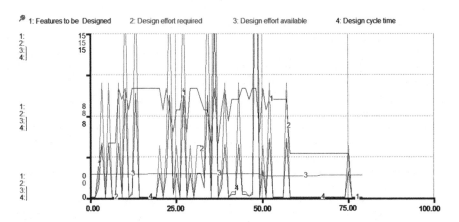

Fig. 6.16 Process model results—highly resource constrained scenario, design view

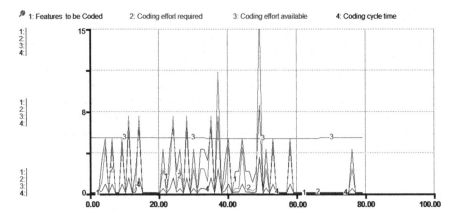

Fig. 6.17 Process model results—highly resource constrained scenario, coding view

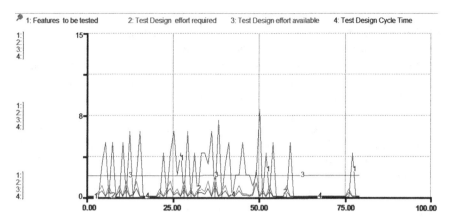

Fig. 6.18 Process model results—highly resource constrained scenario, test design view

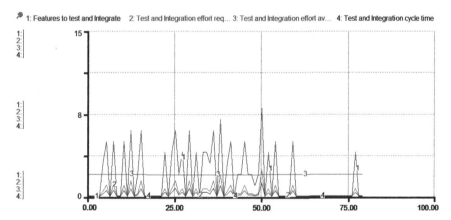

Fig. 6.19 Process model results—highly resource constrained scenario, testing and integration view

General Observations

As a general note, in the real world it is not possible or even desirable to have the exact number of resources available as the model requires for several reasons:

- It is not typically possible to hire fractional resources on a project. Most projects hire dedicated whole resources for a given duration during a project.
- Even if you could hire fractional resources to exactly match the Resources Required, the results would be a much less effective staffing model as any unexpected delays, additional work introduces or changes in staffing profiles, would leave the project in a much less resilient to these changes.

- The pathological work flow 'spikyness' introduced by an imbalance between Effort Required and Effort Available introduces inefficiencies that ultimately result in a longer overall delay to the project than expected.
- Ultimately the cost of the early resource constraint is much more significant than the original delay. For example, a the early delay in resources—say 2 resources over 4 weeks (or 8 staff weeks) caused a delay of 10 weeks for 10 or more staff members (or 100 staff weeks of extra effort)!
- These kinds of interactions are not possible to predict or quantify with traditional models. The hybrid approach of using granular parametric models with process workflow simulations provided insights that were not visible using other techniques.

Chapter 7
Conclusions and Recommendations

How Can You Put These Tools into Practice?

Up to now, tools have been fragmented and non-uniform. As of this writing, a concise version of tools to perform the various analysis described in this document have been written in Python 2.6 with an interface to Excel for data input and output.

The following Python programs are available for limited use and are currently being tested and benchmarked at several organizations including: a major stock exchange, a large media company and a large private University:

Prioritize.py—loads data from an Excel workbook which contains all of the possible strategic objectives that the organization wants to rank. In practice it is desirable to prioritize no more than 10–15 simultaneous objectives—though the technology could easily handle many times more. The reason is that it simply becomes difficult to act on more than that. If we were to prioritize 100 objectives, the result would be many statistical ties which would provide no guidance value. The results of the prioritization algorithm are written back to the Excel workbook.

Rank.py—loads data from the Excel workbook containing the projects or programs which we want to rank against the prioritized strategic objectives. Again, trying to rank hundreds of projects simultaneously would provide little guidance value [41]. The way around this is to treat project groups as investment Tranches and rank those. The results are then written back to an Excel worksheet.

Optimize.py—loads the ranked projects and from the Excel workbook and calculates the aggregate strategic value of each possible grouping. This calculation is performed for every possible combination. The result is a graph which contains an Efficient Frontier [40] analysis that allows one to select the optimal portfolio which provides the most strategic lift for the investment level selected. The results are also written back to an Excel worksheet.

Simulate.py—this program is a little more complex. It reads a process network representation from a spreadsheet, calculates the transfer functions (which determine transit time for each node), loads the work queues into the appropriate node

P. J. Morales and D. Anderson, *Process Simulation and Parametric Modeling for Strategic Project Management*, SpringerBriefs in Electrical and Computer Engineering, DOI: 10.1007/978-1-4614-6989-6_7, © The Author(s) 2013

and then runs a simulation of work flowing through the process network. The result can be calculated in two modes

- unconstrained resource mode: calculates the required resource level required at each node over the 'duration' of the project and gives you an 'ideal' staffing model
- constrained resource mode: allows you to select the resource level at each node for the 'duration' of the project.

The resulting 'minimum' time and effort to complete the work is what would be required if there were no surprises. It may be better to staff defensively for critical nodes in the process which would make the overall staffing plan much more resilient to the risk of losing a staff member or being hit by additional unexpected work.

Python Code

This section contains simplified versions of the Python code. More detailed working versions are available upon request.

```python
# Optimize.py - Copyright 2012 - This software is the property of Dr Peter J Morales
# You have the right to use this software for your own purposes but please
# do not give it to anyone without the knowledge and permission of the author.

#Version 3.2

from PyWorkbooks.ExWorkbook import ExWorkbook
from operator import itemgetter, attrgetter
import string
import types
import time
import sys

class  Strategy:
    def __init__(self):
        self.Dimension = 0
        self.Objective = ""
        self.Comparisons = []
        self.ObjectiveSum = 0.0
        self.ComparisonSum = 0.0
        self.NormalizedSum = 0.0
        self.TotalNormalizedSum = 0.0
        self.FocusPercent = 0.0
        self.Rank = 0
```

```python
def add(self, element):
    if (type(element[0]) != types.NoneType) and (len(element)>2):
        if verbose: print "adding:", element[0], "length-",len(element)
        self.Objective = element[0]
        for i in range(1, len(element)):
            if (element[i] != types.NoneType) :
                self.Comparisons.append(self.convert(str(element[i])))
            else:
                self.Comparisons.append(0)
            if (i > self.Dimension) and (type(element[i]) != types.NoneType):
                self.Dimension = i


def display(self):
    print ""
    print self.Objective, ":",
    print self.Comparisons,
    print self.Dimension,
    print self.Rank
    time.sleep(1)


def convert(self, text_version):
    if verbose: print "converting:", text_version,
    if ('is extremely less important than' in text_version.lower()):
        if verbose: print " = 0.1"
        return 0.1
    elif ('is much less important than' in text_version.lower()):
        if verbose: print " = 0.3"
        return 0.3
    elif ('is less important than' in text_version.lower()):
        if verbose: print " = 0.6"
        return 0.6
    elif ('is as important as' in text_version.lower()):
        if verbose: print " = 1.0"
        return 1.0
    elif ('is more important than' in text_version.lower()):
        if verbose: print " = 3.0"
        return 3.0
    elif ('is much more important than' in text_version.lower()):
        if verbose: print " = 6.0"
        return 6.0
```

```python
      elif ('is extremely more important than' in text_version.lower()):
        if verbose: print " = 9.0"
        return 9.0
      else :
        if verbose: print " = 0"
        return 0


  def invert(self, value):
    if verbose: print "inverting:", value,
    if (value == 0.1):
      if verbose: print " = 9.0"
      return 9.0
    elif (value == 0.3):
      if verbose: print " = 6.0"
      return 6.0
    elif (value == 0.6):
      if verbose: print " = 3.0"
      return 3.0
    elif (value == 1.0):
      if verbose: print " = 1.0"
      return 1.0
    elif (value == 3.0):
      if verbose: print " = 0.6"
      return 0.6
    elif (value == 6.0):
      if verbose: print " = 0.3"
      return 0.3
    elif (value == 9.0):
      if verbose: print " = 0.1"
      return 0.1
    else :
      if verbose: print " = 0"
      return 0


class StrategyMatrix:
  def __init__(self, name):
    self.Name = name
    self.MaxDim = 0
    self.TotalNormalizedSum = 0.0
    self.Strategy = []
```

```python
    def add(self, element):
        if (type(element[0]) != types.NoneType):
            if verbose: print "adding element", element
            thisObj = Strategy()
            thisObj.add(element)
            self.Strategy.append(thisObj)

    def load(self, aPage):
        for element in aPage:
            if verbose : print "loading", element
            self.add(element)

    def display(self):
        print "Strategy", self.Name,
        print "Dimension", self.MaxDim
        for i in range(0, len(self.Strategy)):
            self.Strategy[i].display(),
        print ""

class  Project:
    def __init__(self):
        self.Name = ""
        self.Dimension = 0
        self.StrategicValue = []
        self.StrategicSum = 0.0
        self.PercentValue = 0

    def add(self, element):
        if (type(element[0]) != types.NoneType) and (len(element)>2):
            if verbose: print "adding:", element[0], "length-",len(element)
            self.Name = element[0]
            for i in range(1, len(element)):
                if (element[i] != types.NoneType) :
                    self.StrategicValue.append(self.convert(str(element[i])))
                if (i > self.Dimension) and (type(element[i]) != types.NoneType):
                    self.Dimension = i

    def convert(self, text_version):
        if verbose: print "converting:", text_version,
        if ('extreme' in text_version.lower()):
            if verbose: print " = 9.0"
            return 9.0
```

```
        elif ('strong' in text_version.lower()):
            if verbose: print " = 6.0"
            return 6.0
        elif ('moderate' in text_version.lower()):
            if verbose: print " = 3.0"
            return 3.0
        elif ('low' in text_version.lower()):
            if verbose: print " = 1.0"
            return 1.0
        elif ('none' in text_version.lower()):
            if verbose: print " = 0.0"
            return 0.0
        elif ('no rating' in text_version.lower()):
            if verbose: print " = 0.0"
            return 0.0
        else :
            if verbose: print " = 0"
            return 0


    def display(self):
        print ""
        print self.Name, ":",
        print self.Dimension,
        print self.StrategicValue,
        print self.StrategicSum
        time.sleep(1)


class ProjectMatrix:
    def __init__(self, name):
        self.Name = name
        self.MaxDim = 0
        self.TotalStrategicSum = 0.0
        self.Projects = []


    def add(self, element):
        if (type(element[0]) != types.NoneType):
            if verbose: print "adding element", element
            thisObj = Project()
            thisObj.add(element)
            self.Projects.append(thisObj)
```

```python
def load(self, aPage):
    for element in aPage:
        if verbose : print "loading", element
        self.add(element)


    def display(self):
        print "Name", self.Name,
        print "Dimension", self.MaxDim
        for i in range(0, len(self.Projects)):
            self.Projects[i].display(),
        print ""


if (len(sys.argv) > 0) and (type(sys.argv[1])!= types.NoneType):
    fileName = sys.argv[1]
    print "Opening file:", fileName
else:
    fileName = 'Strategic_Alignment.xlsx'


# Open the Excel workbook
B = ExWorkbook()
B.change_workbook(fileName)
B.change_sheet(0)


vs = B['B1']
if (type(vs)!= types.NoneType) and ('y' in vs.lower()):
    verbose = 1
    print "Running in verbose mode"
else:
    verbose = 0


strategyName = B['B2']
if (type(strategyName)== types.NoneType): strategyName = 'Strategic Alignment'

myPage = B['B3:M20']


myStrategies = StrategyMatrix(strategyName)
myStrategies.load(myPage)
if verbose: myStrategies.display()
```

```
if verbose: print "CALCULATING DIMENSION:",
for i in range(0, len(myStrategies.Strategy)):
  if (myStrategies.Strategy[i].Dimension > myStrategies.MaxDim):
    myStrategies.MaxDim = myStrategies.Strategy[i].Dimension
if verbose: print myStrategies.MaxDim


if verbose: print "CALCULATING RESULTS:",
if verbose: print myStrategies.Name,
for i in range(0, myStrategies.MaxDim):
  if verbose: print myStrategies.Strategy[i].Objective,
  myStrategies.Strategy[i].ObjectiveSum = 0
  for j in range(0, myStrategies.Strategy[i].Dimension):
    if (myStrategies.Strategy[i].Comparisons[j] == 0.0):
      myStrategies.Strategy[i].Comparisons[j] =
myStrategies.Strategy[i].invert(myStrategies.Strategy[j].Comparisons[i])
    if verbose: print myStrategies.Strategy[i].Comparisons[j],
    myStrategies.Strategy[i].ObjectiveSum +=
myStrategies.Strategy[i].Comparisons[j]
  if verbose: print myStrategies.Strategy[i].ObjectiveSum,


B.change_sheet(1)
B[0,0] = myStrategies.Name
for i in range(0, myStrategies.MaxDim):
  B[i+1,0] = myStrategies.Strategy[i].Objective
  for j in range(0, myStrategies.Strategy[i].Dimension):
    if i == 0: B[0,j+1] = myStrategies.Strategy[j].Objective
    B[i+1, j+1] = myStrategies.Strategy[i].Comparisons[j]
    myStrategies.Strategy[i].ComparisonSum +=
myStrategies.Strategy[j].Comparisons[i]


for i in range(0, myStrategies.MaxDim):
  B[myStrategies.MaxDim + 1, i+1] = myStrategies.Strategy[i].ComparisonSum


if verbose: print "CALCULATING NORMALIZED RESULTS"
for i in range(0, myStrategies.MaxDim):
  B[myStrategies.MaxDim+3+i,0] = myStrategies.Strategy[i].Objective
  for j in range(0, myStrategies.Strategy[i].Dimension):
    B[myStrategies.MaxDim+3+i, j+1] =
myStrategies.Strategy[i].Comparisons[j]/myStrategies.Strategy[j].ComparisonSum
    myStrategies.Strategy[i].NormalizedSum +=
```

```
myStrategies.Strategy[i].Comparisons[j]/myStrategies.Strategy[j].ComparisonSum
   myStrategies.Strategy[i].TotalNormalizedSum +=
myStrategies.Strategy[i].NormalizedSum
   B[myStrategies.MaxDim+3+i, myStrategies.Strategy[i].Dimension+1] =
myStrategies.Strategy[i].TotalNormalizedSum
   myStrategies.TotalNormalizedSum +=
myStrategies.Strategy[i].TotalNormalizedSum
B[2*myStrategies.MaxDim+3, myStrategies.MaxDim+1] =
myStrategies.TotalNormalizedSum


for i in range(0, myStrategies.MaxDim):
   B[myStrategies.MaxDim+3+i, myStrategies.Strategy[i].Dimension+2] =
myStrategies.Strategy[i].TotalNormalizedSum / myStrategies.TotalNormalizedSum


if verbose: print "CALCULATING PROJECT ALIGNMENT"
B.change_sheet(2)


projectsName = B['B2']
if (type(projectsName)== types.NoneType): projectsName = 'Project Alignment'


myPage = B['B3:M20']


myProjects = ProjectMatrix(projectsName)
myProjects.load(myPage)
if verbose: myProjects.display()


if verbose: print "CALCULATING PROJECT DIMENSION:",
myProjects.MaxDim = len(myProjects.Projects)
if verbose: print myProjects.MaxDim

B.change_sheet(3)
if verbose: print "CALCULATING PROJECT ALIGNMENT:",
if verbose: print myProjects.Name,
B[0,0] = myProjects.Name
for i in range(0, myProjects.MaxDim):
   if verbose: print myProjects.Projects[i].StrategicValue,
   myProjects.Projects[i].StrategicSum = 0
   B[i+1,0] = myProjects.Projects[i].Name
```

```
   for j in range(0, myStrategies.MaxDim):
     if i == 0: B[0,j+1] = myStrategies.Strategy[j].Objective
     projValue =
myProjects.Projects[i].StrategicValue[j]*(myStrategies.Strategy[j].TotalNormalizedSum
/myStrategies.TotalNormalizedSum)
     B[i+1, j+1] = projValue
     if verbose: print projValue,
     myProjects.Projects[i].StrategicSum += projValue
   if verbose: print myProjects.Projects[i].StrategicSum,


for i in range(0, myProjects.MaxDim):
  B[i+1, myProjects.Projects[i].Dimension+1] = myProjects.Projects[i].StrategicSum
  myProjects.TotalStrategicSum += myProjects.Projects[i].StrategicSum


for i in range(0, myProjects.MaxDim):
  myProjects.Projects[i].PercentValue =
myProjects.Projects[i].StrategicSum/myProjects.TotalStrategicSum
  B[i+1, myProjects.Projects[i].Dimension+2] = myProjects.Projects[i].PercentValue


# Simulate.py – Version 2.01


# Copyright 2012 – This software is the property of Dr Peter J Morales
# You have the right to use this software for your own purposes but please
# do not give it to anyone without the knowledge and permission of the author.


from PyWorkbooks.ExWorkbook import ExWorkbook
import string
import types
import time


class QueueItem:
    def __init__(self, element):
        if (type(element) != types.NoneType):
            self.Magnitude  = element[0]
            self.Complexity = element[1]
            self.Vector     = element[0]*element[1]
            self.Index      = int(element[2])
        else:
            self.Magnitude  = 0
            self.Complexity = 0
            self.Vector     = 0
            self.Index      = 0
```

```python
    def display(self):
        print self.Magnitude,
        print self.Complexity,
        print self.Vector,
        print self.Index

class BacklogQueue:
    def __init__(self, name):
        self.Name = name
        self.Q = []
    def load(self, aPage):
        if verbose: print "loading queue",
        for element in aPage:
            if verbose: print element
            if ((type(element) != types.NoneType) and type(element[0]) !=
types.NoneType):
                aQItem = QueueItem(element)
                self.Q.append(aQItem)
    def get(self, index):
        subQ = []
        for item in self.Q:
            if item.Index == index:
                subQ.append(item)
                return (subQ)
    def get_vector(self, index):
        for item in self.Q:
            if item.Index == index:
                return (item.Vector)
    def display(self):
        print self.Name
        for item in self.Q:
            self.Q.display()

class Node:
    def __init__(self):
        self.Name = ""
        self.ID = 0
        self.TransferFunction = 0
        self.WIP = 0
        self.WC = 0
        self.InQ = []
        self.LinkTo = []
```

```python
def add(self, element, aQueue):
    self.Name = element[0]
    if verbose: time.sleep(1); print "Adding ", self.Name, "[",
    self.ID = int(element[1])
    if verbose: print self.ID, "]",
    if (type(element[2]) != types.NoneType):
        self.WIP = int(element[2])
    else:
        self.WIP = 0
    print " WIP = ", self.WIP,
    if (type(element[3]) != types.NoneType):
        self.TransferFunction = element[3]
    else:
        self.TransferFunction = 0
    self.WC = 0
    # load initial inbound queue
    if verbose: print " loading inbound queues.."
    subQ = aQueue.get(self.ID)
    if (type(subQ) != types.NoneType) and len(subQ)>0:
        for item in subQ:
            if (type(item.Index) != types.NoneType):
                self.InQ.append(int(item.Vector))
                if verbose: print "appending - ", item.Index, ":", item.Vector
    #load transfer function
    if verbose: print self.TransferFunction, " link to-> ",
    if (type(element) != types.NoneType):
        for n in range(4, len(element)):
            if (type(element[n]) != types.NoneType):
                self.LinkTo.append(int(element[n]))
                if verbose: print int(element[n]), ",",
    else:
        self.LinkTo = []
    print ""
def display(self):
    print ""
    print "Display", self.Name,
    print self.ID,
    print self.InQ,
    print self.TransferFunction,
    for n in range(0, len(self.LinkTo)):
        print self.LinkTo[n],
    print ""
    time.sleep(1)
```

```python
class Network:
    def __init__(self, name):
        self.name = name
        self.Nodes = []
    def add(self, element, aQueue):
        if (type(element[0]) != types.NoneType):
            thisNode = Node()
            thisNode.add(element, aQueue)
            self.Nodes.append(thisNode)
    def load(self, aPage, aQueue):
        for element in aPage:
            self.add(element, aQueue)
    def display(self):
        print "Network", self.name,
        for item in self.Nodes:
            item.display()
        print ""


# Define default operating variables
resolution_interval = 100


# Open the Excel workbook
B = ExWorkbook()
B.change_workbook('TestNetwork.xls')


# Load operating overrides from Excel workbook
B.change_sheet(0)
resolution_interval = int(B['B2:B2'])
print "override ri: ", resolution_interval


#load verbose setting
verbose = 0
vs = B['B3:B3']
if (type(vs)!= types.NoneType):
    vs = string.upper(vs)
    if ('Y' in vs):
        verbose = 1


# Load initial backlog queue – into first node by default
myPage = B['B5:D20']
myQueue = BacklogQueue("MyQueue")
myQueue.load(myPage)
if verbose: print"inbound queue:", myQueue.display; time.sleep(5)
```

```python
# Load Process Network Model
B.change_sheet(1)
myPage = B['A2:M50']


myNetwork = Network('testNetwork')
myNetwork.load(myPage, myQueue)
if verbose: myNetwork.display(); time.sleep(5)


results_array=[['Time', 'Node ID', 'WIP', 'WC', 'TF','InQ']]

# iterate time through the rosultion interval (maximum time)
for t in range(0, resolution_interval):
    # iterate through all the nodes
    for n in range(0, len(myNetwork.Nodes)):
        status = "node: "+str(n)
        # if there is no work in process in this node...
        if (myNetwork.Nodes[n].WIP == 0):
            status += " no WIP "+ str(myNetwork.Nodes[n].WIP)
            # ...load work in process from the inbound queue
            if (type(myNetwork.Nodes[n].InQ)!= types.NoneType and
len(myNetwork.Nodes[n].InQ) >= 1):
                myNetwork.Nodes[n].WIP = myNetwork.Nodes[n].InQ.pop(0)
                myNetwork.Nodes[n].WC  = 0
                status += " new WIP "+ str(myNetwork.Nodes[n].WIP)


        # if work left to complete...
        if (myNetwork.Nodes[n].WIP > 0):
            # ... calculate additional work completed
            myNetwork.Nodes[n].WC += myNetwork.Nodes[n].TransferFunction


        #calculate work left in this node
        status += " work left: "+ str(myNetwork.Nodes[n].WIP -
myNetwork.Nodes[n].WC)


        if ((myNetwork.Nodes[n].WIP - myNetwork.Nodes[n].WC) <=
myNetwork.Nodes[n].TransferFunction):
            # ... otherwise send the work downstream to the next available node
            for m in range(0, len(myNetwork.Nodes[n].LinkTo)):
                if (type(myNetwork.Nodes[int(myNetwork.Nodes[n].LinkTo[m])])!=
types.NoneType):
```

```
myNetwork.Nodes[int(myNetwork.Nodes[n].LinkTo[m])].InQ.append(myNetwork.Node
s[n].WIP)
            status += " work pushed to next open link node " +
str(myNetwork.Nodes[n].LinkTo[m])
            myNetwork.Nodes[n].WIP = 0
            #myNetwork.Nodes[n].WC  = 0
            break

    status += " work left "+ str(myNetwork.Nodes[n].WIP)
    status += " trans func "+ str(myNetwork.Nodes[n].TransferFunction)
    status += " work completed "+ str(myNetwork.Nodes[n].WC)

    if (verbose):
       print status
    else:
       status = ""

    # save results
    results_array.append([int(t),
       myNetwork.Nodes[n].ID,
       myNetwork.Nodes[n].WIP,
       myNetwork.Nodes[n].WC,
       myNetwork.Nodes[n].TransferFunction,
       len(myNetwork.Nodes[n].InQ),
       status
       ])

# Write results matrix to Excel worksheet
B.change_sheet(2)
B[0,0] = results_array
```

About the Authors

Dr. Peter J. Morales (Lead Author) is currently working with NYU in various roles with the Law School, the Global University and the CIO Council. Previous roles include CIO of Polytechnic Institute as it joined NYU as the Engineering School. Peter holds a Doctorate in Computer Science and Information Systems from Pace University, a Masters of Science in Management from the Polytechnic Institute of NYU and a Bachelors of Science in Electrical Engineering from the Rochester Institute of Technology. Peter also consults for the City of NY teaching project management to a broad group of managers in city government including the departments of Fire, Police, Corrections, Office of the Budget, DCAS, Parks and others. Prior to NYU, worked in the financial services industry leading technology projects for the American and New York Stock Exchanges. Peter started his career in the Defense world developing Navy avionics diagnostic and information management systems for various platforms including the F18.

Dr. Dennis Anderson is Chair and Professor of Management and Information Technology at St. Francis College. Prior to this appointment he was a Professor of Information Systems and Computer Science and served as Associate Dean at Pace University. He is a strong advocate of technology-enhanced learning, emerging technologies, sustainable technologies, and knowledge entrepreneurship. He also has taught at NYU, City University of New York, and Pace University. Dennis received his Ph.D., M.Phil. and Ed.M. from Columbia University. In addition, he holds an M.S. in Computer Science from NYU's Courant Institute of Mathematical Sciences. For full bio, visit http://www.drdennisanderson.com

P. J. Morales and D. Anderson, *Process Simulation and Parametric Modeling for Strategic Project Management*, SpringerBriefs in Electrical and Computer Engineering, DOI: 10.1007/978-1-4614-6989-6, © The Author(s) 2013

References

1. Archer, N.P., Ghasemzadeh, F. "An integrated framework for Project Portfolio Management" International Journal of Project Management, Vol. 17, No.4
2. Anda, B., Sjøberg, D., and Jørgensen, M. "Quality and Understandability in Use Case Models" Proc. 13th European Conference on Object-Oriented Programming (ECOOP'2001). 2001
3. Arnold, P. and Pedross, P. "Software Size Measurement and Productivity Rating in a Large-Scale Software Development Department. Forging New Links." IEEE Comput. Soc, Los Alamitos, CA, USA, pp. 490–493. 1998.
4. Bednar J. A., Robertson D. "Estimating Size and Effort" University of Edinburgh, Old College South Bridge, Edinburgh EH8 9YL
5. Benaroch M., Kauffman R. "A case for using option pricing analysis to evaluate information technology project investments." Information Systems Research, vol 10, 1999
6. F. Black and M. S. Scholes. "The pricing of options and corporate liabilities". Journal of Political Economy, 81(3):637–54, May–June 1973
7. Boehm, Barry W., "Software Engineering Economics", Prentice Hall, 1981.
8. Boehm, Barry W., Bradford, Clark, et.al."An Overview of the COCOMO 2.0 Software Cost Model", Proceedings of the Software Technology Conference, 1995.
9. Boehm, Barry; Abts, Chris "Software Development Cost Estimation Approaches—A Survey", University of Southern California, Los Angeles, CA 90089-0781
10. Boehm, Barry W., Turner, R. "Balancing Agility and Discipline", Addison Wesley, 2003.
11. Bradley, Ken, "SPOCE Project Management Limited", 2002.
12. Salvatore Cannella and Elena Ciancimino "Capacity constrained supply chains: a simulation study" International Journal of Simulation and Process Modeling, Vol. 4, No. 2, 2008 139
13. "2009 CHAOS Demographics and Project Resolution" Standish Group Quarterly Report, 2009
14. Cohen, D., Lindvall, M., Costa, P. "An Introduction to Agile Methods", Fraunhoffer Center for Experimental Software engineering College Park, MD 20742
15. "Data and Analysis Center for Software report D016" DoD Software Information Clearing House, Rome Air Force Base, Rome, New York, http://www.dacsstore.com/info.php.
16. "Value of commercial software development under technology risk." The financier, 2001
17. Eveleens, J. Laurenz and Verhoef, Chris "The Rise and Fall of the Chaos Report Figures", IEEE Software. February 2010
18. Favaro J., Plfeeger S. "Making software development investment decisions.", Software Engineering Notes, vol. 25, 1998
19. Favaro J., Favaro K., "Strategic analysis of application framework investments.", Building Application Frameworks: Object Oriented Foundations of Framework Design. John Wiley and Sons, 1999

P. J. Morales and D. Anderson, *Process Simulation and Parametric Modeling for Strategic Project Management*, SpringerBriefs in Electrical and Computer Engineering, DOI: 10.1007/978-1-4614-6989-6, © The Author(s) 2013

20. Fetcke. T., Abran, A. and Nguyen, T.-H. "Mapping the OO-Jacobson Approach into Function Point Analysis. International Conference on Technology of Object-Oriented Languages and Systems (TOOLS-23).", IEEE Comput. Soc, Los Alamitos, CA, USA, pp. 192–202. 1998.
21. Fischman, Lee; McRitchie, Karen; and Galorath, Daniel "Inside SEER-SEM", CROSSTALK The Journal of Defense Software Engineering. April 2005
22. Forrester, Jay "The Beginning of System Dynamics" Banquet Talk at the international meeting of the System Dynamics Society. Stuttgart, Germany. July 13, 1989
23. Forrester, Malcom, "How Do Simple Rules 'Fit to Reality' in a Complex World?" Minds and Machines 9: 543–564
24. B Gallagher "The Rational Unified Process and the CMM Systems/Software Engineering", Carnegie Mellon University Press, 2001
25. Gigerenzer, G., Todd, "Simple heuristics that make us smart." Oxford University Press. 1999
26. Hansman, John "Identification of Inter-facility Communication and Coordination in the US Air Traffic Control System", Report to the National Science Foundation and the Ames Research Center under Grant NAG 2-1299. 2001
27. Jacobson, Ivar "Object Oriented Software Engineering—A Use Case Driven Approach", 1992
28. Jacobsen, Ivar; Booch, Grady; Rumbaugh, James "The Unified Software Development Process", Addison Wesley. 1999
29. Jensen, R.W. and Tonies, C.C. "Software Engineering", Prentice Hall, Englewood Cliffs N.J. 1979
30. Jones, Capers "Estimating Software Costs: bringing realism to estimating", McGraw-Hill Prof Med/Tech, 2007
31. Huang J. C "Software Cost Estimation presentation", Department of Computer Science. University of Houston. 2005
32. Highsmith J. "Adaptive Software Development", Dorset House Publishing, 1999
33. Carl Gustav Jung. "Psychological Types, volume 6 of The collected works of C. G. Jung", Princeton University Press, 1971.
34. Jaswinder Kaur, Satwinder Singh, and Karanjeet Singh Kahlon "Comparative Analysis of the Software Effort Estimation Models", Princeton University Press, 1971. World Academy of Science, Engineering and Technology 46 2008
35. Karner, G. "Metrics for Objectory". Diploma thesis, University of Linköping, Sweden. No. LiTHIDA-Ex-9344:21. December 1993.
36. Kuhn, Thomas "The structure of scientific revolution (2nd ed.).", University of Chicago Press, 1970
37. Lewis, J. P. "Large Limits to Software Estimation", ACM Software Engineering Notes Vol 26, No. 4 July 2001 p. 54–59
38. Xiaotong Li, University of Alabama in Huntsville John D. Johnson, University of Mississippi "Evaluate IT Investment Opportunities Using Real Options Theory", Information resources Management Journal, 15(3), 32–47, July–Sept. 2002
39. Lueherman, Timothy "Strategy as a Portfolio of Real Options", Harvard Business Review. September–October 1998
40. Markowitz, H. M. "Portfolio Selection : Efficient Diversification of Investments", New York, New York. John Wiley and Sons, 1959
41. Martino, Joseph P. "R & D Project Selection", New York, New York John Wiley and Sons, 1995.
42. "The project management body of knowledge, 3rd edition" Project Management Institute Press, 2004
43. Putnam L., Myers W. "Five Core Metrics: The intelligence behind successful software management.", Dorset House Publishing, 2003.
44. Seigelaub, J. "How Prince2 can compliment PMBOK and your PMP.", PMI Global Conference Proceedings. PMI Press. 2006.

45. Sendall, S. and Stroheimer, A. "From Use Cases to System Operation Specification.", Third International Conference on the Unified Modeling Language (UML'2000), York, UK. LNCS1939; Springer Verlag, pp. 1–15. 2000.

46. Shumsky, Robert A. "A Note on Project Scheduling", William E. Simon Graduate School of Business Administration. University of Rochester, July 24, 2003

47. Yuki Sugiyama, Minoru Fukui, Macoto Kikuchi, et. al. "Traffic jams without bottlenecks—experimental evidence for the physical mechanism of the formation of a jam.", The new journal of physics, IOP Publishing Ltd and Deutsche Physikalische Gesellschaft 2008

48. Sullivan K "Software design: the options approach." SIGSOFT Architectures Workshop, San Francisco, California, 1996

49. Tansey, Brendan and Stroulia, Eleni "Valuating Software Service Development: Integrating COCOMO II and Real Options Theory", Department of Computing Science, University of Alberta, Edmonton, AB, T6G 2E8, Canada, 2009

50. Wiegers, Karl E. "Stop Promising Miracles", Software Development, February 2000

51. Wiegers, Karl E. "10 Requirements Traps to Avoid", Software Testing & Quality Engineering, January/February 2000

52. Williams, L, "A Survey of Agile Development Methodologies", North Carolina State University. 2007